# Emotions in Wood

GH00808950

Linden Publishing

Fresno

# Emotions
# in Wood

## Carving the Expressive Face

Ann Brouwers

For Dennis!

May this book inspire you
to make a lot of beautiful
sculptures. And if you have
a question, just e-mail me:
houtvanann @ hotmail . com

xxx
Ann

# Emotions in Wood

by

## Ann Brouwers

Cover design: James Goold

357986421

ISBN 978-1-933502-16-8

Printed in Thailand


Library of Congress Cataloging-in-Publication Data
Brouwers, Ann, 1963-
  Emotions in wood : carving the expressive face / Ann Brouwers.
    p. cm.
  ISBN-13: 978-1-933502-16-8 (pbk. : alk. paper)
  ISBN-10: 1-933502-16-9 (pbk. : alk. paper)
  1. Wood-carving--Technique. 2. Face in art. 3. Head in art. I. Title.
  TT199.7.B76245 2008
  731.4'62--dc22
                        2008009254

Woodworking is inherently dangerous. Your safety is your responsibility.

Neither Linden Publishing nor the author assume any responsibility

for any injuries or accidents.

## Linden Publishing Inc.
2006 S. Mary
Fresno, CA
www.lindenpub.com
800-345-4447

# Table of Contents

# Introduction

I live near Brussels, the capital of Belgium, a small country in the heart of Europe, with many other nations and languages surrounding it.

I grew up with a love of languages. I studied Dutch, French, English and German in high school, and Arabic and Persian at the University of Louvain. But until about 14 years ago I had no idea that I had not encountered the biggest passion in my life; wood sculpture.

In 1993, when renovating an old house, wood came into my life. I fell in love with wood as a material. Wood, for the windows in pitch pine, the stairs in beech, the floor in oak...

I wanted to learn everything about wood. I studied renovating antique furniture. I completed a course on lutherie (building a violin), and a course on sculpture in wood.

I discovered that I had a talent for sculpture. The combination of a passion for wood and a talent for sculpture give me great satisfaction. It started as a hobby, but grew into something bigger. Sculpting in wood is not just a part of my life, it is my life. It would be impossible for me to stop carving.

After a number of years I started to teach carving. I wanted to share my passion for wood with others. I like to show beginning carvers the best way to get the best results.

I give workshops for small groups, a maximum of six people, so that I can give everyone enough attention. I want students to discover the enormous possibilities of wood and sculpture. I want them to start with enthusiasm, end the course with enthusiasm and go on carving on their own with enthusiasm, preferably for the rest of their lives.

This book offers you a new, contemporary approach to an ancient and beautiful art, the art of woodcarving.

I will show you how you can explore your own creative skills and make a modern, attractive carving.

Wood is one of the most beautiful, versatile, and natural materials on earth. And with some simple tools you can make from this material a work of art.

This book will teach you how to carve a human emotion in an extraordinary, uncommon design. The design is simple and strong, a sphere. Out of the sphere come the face and the emotion. Not a realistic human face, but a face out of your imagination.

Many people consider the human face difficult to carve, and emotions in a face as even more difficult. This book shows you where these difficulties are, and tells you how to tackle them. The difference between a realistic face and a spherical face is explained. You don't have to be able to carve a human face before you carve a spherical head.

Each part of the book shows the carver how to proceed with one emotion. Step-by-step photos and explanations will encourage readers to create their own spherical faces.

And last but not least, a part of this book explains how to do your own creative thinking. You can do even more than just carve. You will find that you can learn how to create your own designs.

*Page 67*

*Page 113*

*Page 111*

*Page 116*

*Page 117*

*Page 116*

*Page 115*

*Page 115*

*Page 93*

Page 116

Carvings by Ann Brouwers

Page 117

Chapter 1

# Choosing your wood

For every design there is the right kind of wood. There is only one problem, how to pick the right kind for your particular sculpture? The world is full of beautiful woods, some of them are good for carving, some of them are even great.

There are some criteria to help you choose. Ask yourself the following questions to establish what kind of wood will be the right one for you.

1. Is the sculpture for interior or exterior use? For example, if you want to put your sculpture in the garden, go for a piece of elm, oak or cedar.

2. Is the sculpture going to be large or small?

Some kinds of wood are very difficult or impossible to find in large dimensions. I like to work in boxwood, a very hard, yellow wood, traditionally used for transverse flutes. However, you will not find many large pieces of boxwood. Furthermore, they are quite expensive. The same holds true for ebony.

3. Are you looking for a special color for your sculpture, or another special effect, inherent in the wood? Yew for example has a beautiful red heart surrounded by white sapwood. Satinwood is yellowish and has a wonderful glow, but is expensive and not always easy to find.

4. Do you prefer the wood to be coarse or fine-grained? For me the answer is easy, fine grained suits my purpose, especially with a spherical form. Fine grain offers a smooth surface and a soft touch.

5. The most important question you

Figure 1. Zebrano (Microberlinia brazzavillensis) *immediately catches the eye.*

*Figure 2. Pear* (Pyrus communis) *has a very fine grain.*

*Figure 3. Black walnut* (Juglans nigra) *has a beautiful dark color.*

have to ask yourself is, what effect do I wish to create? As I mentioned above, for every design there is the right kind of wood. My opinion is that the more you want to draw the attention to the lines you carved, the more you need to choose an inconspicuous kind of wood.

Lime for example is a wood with a very fine, indistinct grain. As a result, in a finished carving, the attention of the observer will be drawn to the carved lines, much less to the character of the wood. Maple or sycamore, both harder than lime, have about the same effect.

If you carve a piece in zebrano the observer will immediately be attracted by the striking alternation of light and dark grain in the wood. Only at a second look will they direct their attention to the carved lines (**Figure 1**).

If you succeed in combining the character of the wood and your carved lines, you will create maximum impact on the spectator. I am not saying that you should never use a strikingly beautiful wood with a lot of character. On the contrary, if you have a beautiful piece, use it, by all means. Just make sure you know what to use it for.

Choose a design fit for the wood you have. If you carve something that has an extremely simple design, choosing a striking piece of wood will enhance the design.

I often use lime, cherry, maple (**Figure 4**), sycamore, pear (**Figure 2**) and European walnut (**Figure 3**) for my spherical heads. For small pieces I also like to work in yew and boxwood. In Europe, butternut, often used in America for carving, is not so easy to find.

For the loudly laughing head I want to draw everyone's attention immediately to the smile, that is, to the mouth and chubby cheeks. I will use a piece of lime. Lime is a great wood to carve, soft but good for details and not so highly figured as to distract observers or take their glance away from the mouth and cheeks.

Figure 4. Maple (Acer) is quite hard but holds detail very well.

Chapter 2

# How to work safely

Figure 5. Pfeil gouges sizes 2/25, 2/35, 7/18.

# Gouges

I carve a spherical head using only gouges. No machines are needed. You do not need to use a lathe to turn your piece of wood into the right dimensions for a spherical head. If you have gouges, you can carve a spherical head.

I like to work with Pfeil gouges, made in Switzerland. Pfeil means Arrow, hence the little arrow on the metal. I also like the American made Flexcut tools very much. Thanks to their flexibility they are great to use in difficult places, in the mouth for example. I also possess some French Auriou gouges that are quite useful.

Gouges come in all sizes and degrees of curvature, or sweep. On each gouge you can find two numbers. Sometimes they are only on the metal, sometimes on the metal and the handle. What do these numbers mean? The first number defines the curvature. It goes from 1, flat, to 11, which is a veiner and has the form of the letter U. 12, 13, 14, 15 and 16 are V-tools. The second number on the gouge is the width in millimeters.

For example, a Pfeil gouge 2/25 is almost flat but not completely and has a width of 25 millimeters, that is, about one inch broad (**Figure 5** and **Figure 6**).

If you work with other makes of gouges do not just look at the numbers on the gouge but also compare the curve, because the numbering is not always the same for all manufacturers (**Figure 7**).

When I write about gouges in this book, I will use the numbers found on the Pfeil gouges. As I go along carving a spherical head I will mention these numbers, so that you know what gouge I used.

# Safety

Gouges need to be extremely sharp in order to do their job and cut the wood correctly. Never underestimate the sharp edges. The rules for safe carving are simple, but you have to stick to them. Working safely has to become an instinct when you are carving.

Always keep your hands behind the edge. Cut away from your body. Never point the gouge in the direction of your body when you carve. This sounds ludicrously easy, but often I notice in my workshops that people are so preoccupied thinking what to cut and where to

Figure 6. An Auriou gouge 6/25 in front and Pfeil gouges 2/25, 2/35, 7/10, 9/7.

cut that they forget their own safety.

If a gouge falls, or should you drop it, do not attempt to pick it up while it is falling. Furthermore, take a step backwards, so that the gouge does not fall on your foot. A gouge can easily cut through shoe leather. Never carve while bare-footed or wearing sandals.

When you are carving take your time to tidy your workspace regularly. It helps if you to have a good overview of the gouges and where they are on the bench. More importantly, you will not cut yourself with the edge of a gouge hidden under chips of wood. I think you can work faster if you take the time to clear your workspace once in a while.

Make sure that your piece of wood is at all times firmly attached in your vise.

When you carve, you combine a physical and mental process. It can be quite tiring if you're working on a new design. When you are tired you will inevitably make mistakes, you can cut yourself or cut away too much wood. Do yourself a favor and take a break once in awhile.

Dust is another health hazard. The dust of some woods, like padouk and mahogany, is poisonous and can cause allergic reactions. Be especially careful when you use machines for sanding. Try to work with a dust extractor. Remember that fine dust particles, smaller than 5 microns, go directly into your lungs via normal respiration.

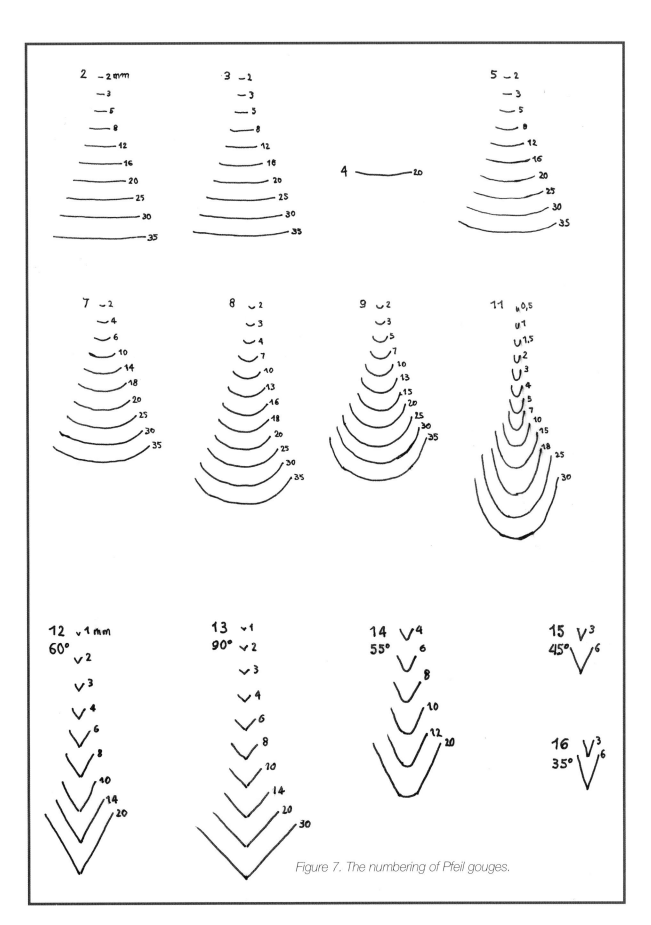

Figure 7. The numbering of Pfeil gouges.

Chapter 3

# *Sharpening*

Carving needs to be done with a very sharp tool. A blunt gouge is dangerous for you and for the quality of your carving. With a blunt tool you can easily lose control over your cutting. You can hurt yourself, you tire yourself needlessly and can make irreparable mistakes.

For a beginning carver sharpening (both grinding and honing) often is a nightmare. How to start? How to find your way among all the different machines, stones, oils?

Traditionally carvers used large grinding wheels, turning in water, and oilstones to sharpen their carving tools. They started on the grinding wheel or on a very coarse stone, then moved on to a finer stone, and finally to a strop to make the edge razor sharp.

In order to have a straight bevel, you must hold your gouge at a constant angle whilst grinding the edge. Holding your tool the whole time at the same, exact angle while moving it back and forth on the oilstone is quite difficult (**Figure 8**).

It is important to know the correct angle at which to hold the tool, 20 degrees is good, up to 25 degrees for rougher work. If you grind your tool at 15 degrees, you get a very thin and very sharp edge. It may serve when you need to do extremely fine work. But a very long bevel is weak and the edge can suddenly break (**Figure 9**).

It is best to grind a tool to serve well for normal work. I suggest you choose a somewhat shorter bevel of 20 degrees (**Figure 10**).

*Figure 8. The gouge hasn't been held at a constant angle to the grinding stone during sharpening. Hence the different planes on the bevel. Furthermore, the bevel is too long for this large gouge (9/30) that is used for rough work.*

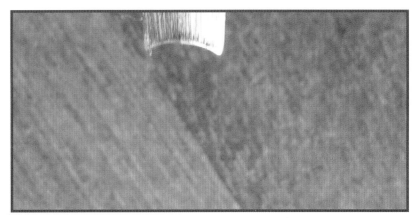

*Figure 9. The bevel is too long, this edge will be fragile.*

*Figure 10. The length of the bevel is correct.*

Figure 11. Here is a Swedish Tormek grinding machine, the light version for the hobbyist. The two thin disks on the left are the profiled leather honing wheels for removing the burr on the inside of a gouge.

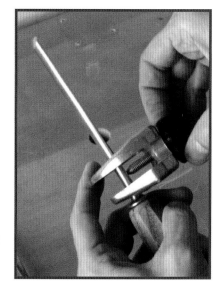

Figure 12. The Tormek device must be screwed on the gouge.

Figure 13. Let the gouge with the metal device lean on the metal support of the machine. You can put the gouge against the wheel, and turn it according to its curvature while at all times your gouge remains at the same angle to the grinding stone. The holding device makes sharpening much easier.

Moving the tool on the stone makes the edge sharp and raises a burr that has to be removed. To remove the burr, use a strop with some stropping paste. This will leave the cutting edge razor sharp. You can make your own strop from a piece of leather fixed with glue.

The strop should always be in reach for immediate and constant use. When a tool has been used some time it becomes slightly dull and a few strokes on the strop will make the edge keen again.

# Modern sharpening methods

The traditional, but quite time-consuming and rather difficult method, can be replaced by modern, powered whetstones, dry or wet grinders. I recommend my students use a Tormek grinding machine. This Swedish-made machine combines sharpening and honing in one machine.

Because the Tormek is water cooled, you don't need to be afraid of the steel becoming overheated. The machine combines a grinding stone (aluminium oxide) on the right side, and a leather-honing wheel on the left. In order to be able to hone and strop the inside of your gouges you need to purchase a profiled leather-honing wheel. This is an additional element of the Tormek system. Tormek also provides accessories that help you hold your gouge at the right angle whilst sharpening (**Figure 11**).

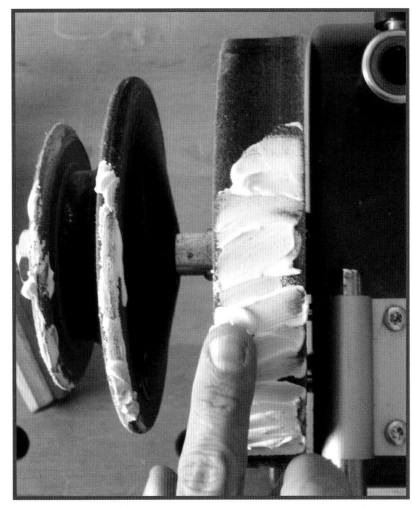

Figure 14. For stropping, apply abrasive paste to the leather wheel.

Figure 15. Remove the burr on the inside and outsideof the gouge.

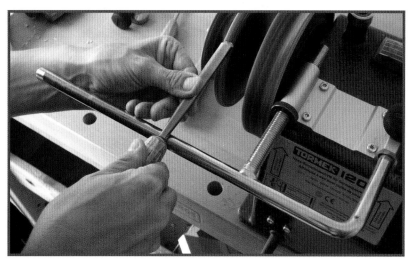

Figure 16. You can reverse the metal support if you prefer a support to lean on.

I use the short tool jig, the SVS-32, which is screwed onto the gouge (**Figure 12**). The Tormek machine has a metal support that can be moved closer or further away from the grinding stone. Put your gouge in the jig on the metal support, look for the right angle. Now fasten the metal support, switch on the machine and turn your gouge against the moving grinding stone. Always keep the jig with the tool firmly on the metal support; this guarantees a consistent angle (**Figure 13**).

You can have a look at what you are doing, feel if there is a burr being raised, and then put back the gouge on the support. Thanks to the grinding jig, the angle will be the same as before and you will end up with a sharp edge.

As soon as you feel a burr all over the edge of the gouge, move on to the leather-honing wheel on the left side of the machine. Apply some abrasive paste to the wheel. Next hone and strop the outside of your gouge on the leather wheel (**Figure 14**). To remove the burr, hone the tool alternately on the inside and outside. Go from the flat leather strop for the outside to the profiled leather disks for the inside of the gouge. Do this often, you needn't be afraid of ruining the bevel. The abrasive paste is not going to change the angle on the bevel (**Figure 15** and **Figure 16**).

This Tormek machine is very effective as long as you never let your gouges deteriorate. An extremely damaged edge will take a lot of time to restore. You need to sharpen very regularly.

If you do that, it will go quickly. Five times of sharpening will take you less time than repairing one badly damaged edge.

# Why so sharp?

The only thing that is indispensable for carving is a sharp tool. A blunt gouge is dangerous for you and for your carving. You can hurt yourself; you tire yourself needlessly, and can make irreparable mistakes. I notice that when people feel they are not being productive, or feel they've lost their drive, the reason is likely to be a blunt tool.

There are a lot of ways to sharpen your gouges. Many carvers have their own tricks. But one thing never changes, practice makes perfect. The more you sharpen the better you get at it and the less time you put into it. It is my experience that most beginners are afraid to sharpen, afraid to make the edge worse than the blunt edge they already have. Beginners have to force themselves, or get forced by others, to start sharpening. I find the Tormek sharpening system a good solution. Thanks to its accessories even a beginner succeeds in sharpening the gouge, and with the right bevel (**Figure 17**).

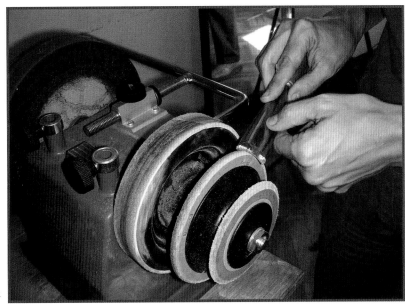

Figure 17. The Tormek strops the gouge. Photograph by Guido Cuyx.

**Tip:** You can start carving with only a couple of gouges, but you cannot start without the stones or machines to sharpen your gouges. What is the use of a blunt gouge? Not being able to sharpen your gouge means you cannot carve.

Chapter 4

# Hand positions

The day I started carving I was really surprised. A gouge has a handle to hold it, but still that is not enough. You have to hold the metal of the gouge too. Use both hands to hold a gouge. One hand has a grip on the handle, the other hand holds the steel close to the handle.

If you are right-handed, put your left hand on the metal, your thumb is pointing towards the handle. The lower part of your left hand almost reaches the point of the tool. Put your right hand around the handle, your thumb is pointing downward. I usually have my index finger pointing to the metal, but this is not a necessity (**Figure 18**).

Your right hand does the pushing while the left hand holds your gouge back and prevents it from slipping.

When I started I learned to work right-handed and left-handed. This allows you to work more freely, just change hands to cut the grain. This means you put your right hand on the metal, the left on the handle.

It is important to let your left hand (for a right-handed person) rest on something. It most often is your piece of wood, but can also be the vise, or workbench, whatever is most convenient. A left-handed person will let his right hand lean on something. This gives you more stability and control over your cuts (**Figure 19**).

Your hands should always be behind the cutting edge. Always cut away from your body. If a place is hard to reach, turn the piece of wood, or turn yourself.

*Figure 18. You use both hands to hold a gouge. One hand has a grip on the handle, the other hand holds the metal close to the handle*

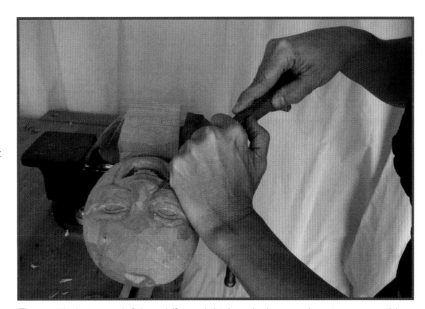

*Figure 19. Let your left hand (for a right-handed person) rest on something.*

If you use a mallet, do not hold the gouge too tightly in your left hand (for a right-handed person). The mallet sits in your right hand. Your left hand points your gouge into the correct direction. Hit the top of the handle while letting the gouge in your left hand do the work.

A mallet is used for hard work and for extremely fine work. If you are afraid to cut away something by pushing too hard with your right hand, use the mallet. With the mallet it is easier to control the length of the cut.

Chapter 5

# Differences between a realistic and a spherical head

Figure 20. A front view of a spherical face in lime. Notice the face is much wider at the eyes and cheeks.

Figure 21. A front view of a realistic face in lime (linden) (Tilia spp).

The global form of a human head is egg shaped. We will carve a round, spherical head. This is the most striking difference between the two, and has some consequences for the human face.

A spherical head is almost realistic, but not completely. You have to know the differences before you start carving.

The spherical head has no ears, no hair and no neck. For a maximum effect the round form has to be absolute. The forehead is part of the sphere and thus loses the frontal eminence. Eyebrows, brow ridges, and the eye cover folds can almost be carved as in a normal head, but there is a difference: because they are part of a sphere, they slope backwards.

The form of the eyes is the same in both faces. But the width of the face at the height of the eyes is larger in a spherical head. This means you have more wood at the outer side of each eye.

The cheekbones of a spherical head are wider than normal and influence the cheeks. For a laughing face this space is great, you can use it for wonderfully chubby cheeks.

The nose and mouth are as realistic as in a normal human head.

But further down, the chin and connection to the cheeks, is different from a normal head. You need to make sure that the chin is not too protruding. If it is you break the spherical form.

You have to stick to the form of the sphere, as much as possible, and at the same time give the sphere as many human traits as possible.

To conclude, there are differences in:

- the forehead,
- the eyes,
- the cheeks,
- the chin.

The spherical head and the human head are the same in the middle:

- the eyebrows near the nose,
- the nose,
- the mouth.

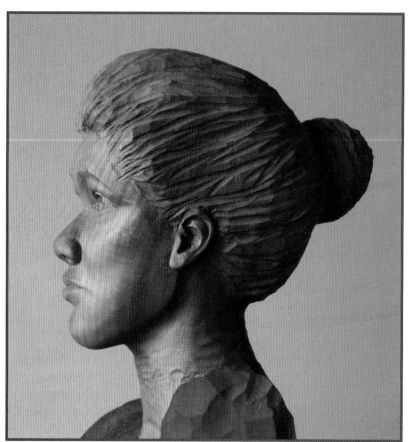

Figure 22. A profile of a realistic face.

Figure 23. A profile of a spherical head. Note the difference in the forehead and chin.

Figure 24. The back of a spherical head. You can see that the sphere is handmade, not turned on a lathe.

**Tip:**

**How to light your subject**

I prefer to work with natural daylight. A clouded sky gives you the best light. The sun on your workbench casts a lot of unwanted shadows.

Shadows on your wood make you see differently, and if you look at your work later, when all shadows have gone, you'll notice mistakes.

The light should never come from behind the workpiece: it puts the wood you need to see in the dark. Nor should it come from behind you, then you cast your own shadow on your work.

Preferably the light comes from a window facing the north. This means no sun, no shadows. I like to work under a window in the roof, the light then seems to come from everywhere. It can also come from your left of right side, or from both sides, even better.

Never use a lamp that casts shadows. A fluorescent lamp is the best option. Buy a good portable lamp, or even two, so you can light your piece from different sides.

Avoid doing your final cuts with electrical light, in the evening. Make sure you have the best daylight (no harsh shadows), it will give you the best final results.

Chapter 6

# The anatomy of the face

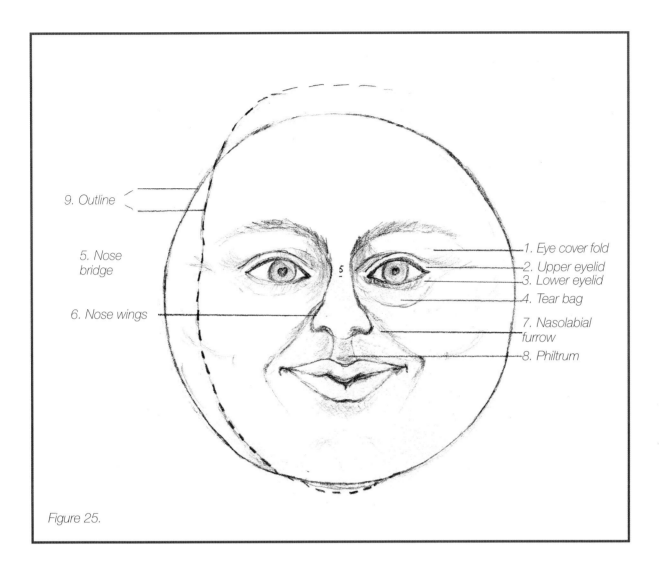

9. Outline

5. Nose bridge

6. Nose wings

1. Eye cover fold
2. Upper eyelid
3. Lower eyelid
4. Tear bag
7. Nasolabial furrow
8. Philtrum

Figure 25.

In a spherical head the facial features look very much the same as in a normal head, which has more or less the form of an egg.

The names of the different parts in a spherical or normal face are of course the same. You will find the names on the drawings (**Figure 25** and **Figure 26**) here and on the next page. I will use these terms throughout the book.

# 1. Eye cover fold

The eye cover fold starts under the eyebrow and hangs down to the upper eyelid. When people get older the eye cover fold sometimes covers the upper eyelid completely, mostly on the outside corners of the eye. In some cases the cover fold hangs over the eye and obstructs vision. If that happens, surgery may be needed to pull the eye cover fold up. I mention this to show you how important the eye cover fold is when you are carving the area above the eye. It is often much more striking than the upper eyelid.

# 2. Upper eyelid

The upper eyelid is partly hidden under the eye cover fold. Still, not carving it would leave a strange impression. For young people, where the skin hasn't started to sag yet, you can see more of the upper eyelid. It follows the form of the eyeball and folds neatly around it. In the corners it touches the lower eyelid. We cannot carve the eyelashes, but we make the eyelids a bit thicker than usual, to give the impression of something more.

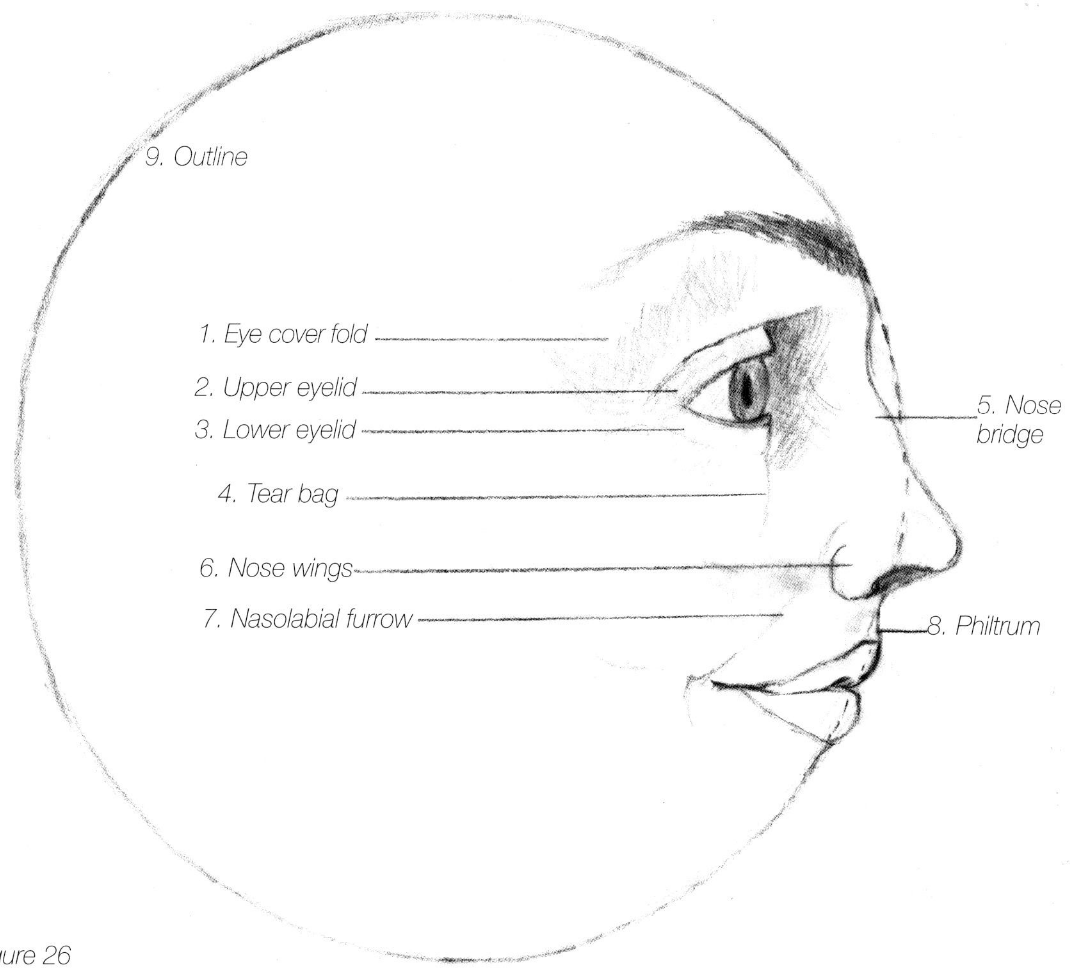

9. Outline

1. Eye cover fold

2. Upper eyelid

3. Lower eyelid

4. Tear bag

6. Nose wings

7. Nasolabial furrow

5. Nose bridge

8. Philtrum

Figure 26

## 3. Lower eyelid

The skin folds around the eyeball and forms the lower eyelid. Our tear ducts end in the upper and lower eyelids. When you cry, the eyelid becomes thicker. Again, on the lower eyelid we cannot carve the eyelashes. Make the lower eyelid a bit thicker than the upper eyelid. You can clearly see the thickness of the lower eyelid, whereas you cannot see it for the upper eyelid. In the profile drawing you see only one line for the upper eyelid, two lines for the lower eyelid.

## 4. Tear bag

The tear bag is not very striking in young people, but more and more visible the older people get. The tear bag is soft tissue and can sag.

## 5. Nose bridge

The bridge is the spot on the nose where the bone is thick. If the nose bridge is very thick, it can give the nose a little bulge and create a characteristic look, though not one most people like.

## 6. Nose wings

The wings of the nose form the left and right side of the nose and are tucked away, quite deeply, in the furrow that lies behind the nose.

# 7. Nasolabial furrow

The nasolabial furrow is very demonstrative and changes with the emotions you feel. It runs down from the nose to the corners of the mouth. It starts just behind the wings of the nose. For a carver, cutting in this furrow means you can start carving the area of the mouth separately from the cheeks.

# 8. Philtrum

The philtrum is a small gully that starts under the nose and ends at the two highest points of the upper lip. Some people have a really deep philtrum, in others the philtrum is hardly noticeable. Still, it is always there. Not carving it would give the immediate impression that something was missing. When you laugh loudly the philtrum disappears, because the muscles around the mouth stretch the skin and pull the philtrum almost completely flat.

# 9. Outline

Notice that a spherical face is broader than a normal face, which affects the cheeks and outside of the eyes. A spherical head is also not as long as a normal face. This means that all the facial features are pressed together in this kind of face.

Chapter 7

# Make a plan

Good preparation is the best path to a beautiful carving. You must know what you are going to do. You need a clear drawing to work with. It need not be a perfect artistic drawing. You do not have to be a gifted or talented painter to draw your own plan. I call it a plan, it is actually your blueprint for your carving.

Just try it. Making a drawing is the very first step to carving. You are working on your carving without even touching a gouge. But you are getting to know your subject, and that is very important. The subject has to be in your head when you begin to carve.

How to start? Take a pencil, and put an eraser nearby. Draw a circle by hand, do not use a compass. It doesn't have to be one perfect line. You can make several attempts and use the eraser for any corrections. Make a nice round form, one you like and that looks circular.

Draw the circle in the exact dimension of the piece of wood you have chosen. In my case it has a diameter of 4½ inches (11.5 cm). You can also draw it at the size you prefer and afterwards make it smaller or larger with the photocopier. After drawing the circle, put a line through the middle. Do it by hand. The more you practice this, the easier it becomes. I prefer to draw the line by hand, because it forces me to make good use of my eyes. Look closely at what you have done, correct yourself, and look again, until you are satisfied.

You need a frontal plan. You also

Figure 27. A simple drawing makes a useful plan.

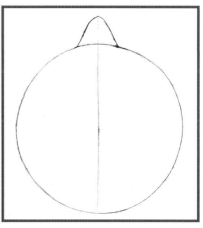

Figure 28. The head as seen from above.

need a second plan, quite easy to draw but very helpful, the head seen from above.

When you laugh a lot of muscles in your face move. The most striking feature in a loudly laughing face is a wide-open mouth. The edges of the mouth go up and the lips part. You always see the upper teeth, and when laughing really loudly, you also see the lower teeth.

The nose broadens, that is, the wings of the nose expand. Stand in front of a mirror, laugh loudly, and look at the changes in your face. The cheeks are being pulled up and cause the eyes to become much smaller than usual. The eyes become slit-eyes showing very little of the pupil. Laugh lines appear at the corners of the eyes.

In a realistic head, the further you open your mouth in a big smile, the more you lower your chin. In fact, your face becomes longer if you laugh loudly. This offers a unique problem because you cannot make a spherical head longer. If you try, you lose the round form. I have solved this by making the forehead

slightly smaller, and I take the extra space for the mouth. Do not forget that the open, laughing mouth will be the first thing that attracts the onlooker's attention. So, be sure to give the mouth all the space it needs, and make a really big mouth.

The muscles around the mouth pull the edges of the mouth backwards and the nasolabial furrow deepens. You can get a secondary little furrow under the cheeks. In some faces the furrow is more like a charming little hole that appears every time the person laughs. Sometimes it appears at both sides, often also only on one side. It is a nice feature to use on your carving.

Chapter 8

# *Preparing the wood*

I selected a piece of lime/linden for my loudly laughing spherical head (**Figure 29**).

After deciding on the kind of wood that you want to use, you need to find a piece fit for use. Watch out for faults, cracks or color changes in a piece, although sometimes I especially look for a crack, a split, or a color change.

When you pick your piece, decide where the face will be. Are there any particular characteristics of the wood you would like to use? If you do not have a lot of experience in woodcarving, go for a flawless piece if possible because it will be much easier to work with.

Make sure you do not select a piece with flaws such as knots or splits in the forehead. A laughing person has no wrinkles or unevenness on his forehead. An uneven rugged forehead makes a big smile look sarcastic or even satanical.

You can choose a piece from a beam at the local lumberyard or a piece from a tree trunk or large branch. However, the easiest way to start is with a square piece of wood that you bought from a reliable wood supply store.

Particulars of a square piece from a lumberyard:

   -good overview of the quality

   -no cracks, no splits

   -no sapwood

   -easy to put your drawing on the square sides of the wood

Particulars of a piece from a stem or branch:

Figure 29. This piece of lime is 13.5 cm thick, 11.5 cm wide and 15 cm long (5 x 4½ x 6 inches).

**Tip:** Never think too far ahead. If you do, you only see problems, and no immediate solutions. You will get stuck, not knowing what to cut away. Tackle one problem at a time. You see some wood that shouldn't be there, remove it. If you work step-by-step, you take on the problems step-by-step. And before you even realize it, the problem has been solved.

*Figure 30. Here we have the finished base. The piece of lime was not quite straight. I made certain that the wood had straight edges before I began work.*

-not so easy to put your drawing on the wood

-you already have a round form

-you need to remove the sapwood and still make room for the nose

-difficult to find without splits

However, the natural branch will always give you a special natural effect, you can almost feel the tree inside the face. For me the natural effect is the main motivation to choose a piece of stem or branch. Nevertheless, my advice is to make your first piece out of a neat, square piece of good quality wood.

The dimensions of my piece are 5 x 4½ x 6 inches high (13.5 cm x 11.5 cm x 15 cm).

## The base

During the whole carving process you need to be able to put the wood firmly in a vise. You can glue an extra piece of wood underneath your workpiece and secure it with a couple of screws. The base should not be too big, otherwise it gets in the way when you need to round the head. An alternative is to buy your wood a bit larger and use part of it as the base. I prefer the latter, because the sphere will always be firmly secured. At the end you just have to remove the base, and there will be no holes left from the screws.

The best form for the base is a square. You need to rotate your piece often and if the base is square you don't have to open and close the vise each time.

My piece of wood is rectangular, 5 x 4½ x 6 inches (13.5 cm x 11.5 cm x 15 cm high). I need a square for the sphere plus extra wood for the nose. I can make a sphere with a diameter of 4½ inches (11.5 cm), which leaves ⅞ inch (2 cm) for the nose (**Figure 30**).

Therefore I made a drawing, front view, of a spherical head with a diameter of 4½ inches. I also made a drawing of the spherical head as seen from the top, with a diameter of 4½ inches, plus the protruding nose of ¾ inch (2 cm).

As my piece of lime is 6 inches (15 cm) in height, and I only need 4½ inches (11.5 cm) for the head, so I can use 1⅜ inches (3.5 cm) for the base.

Mark the correct distance, 4½ inches (11.5 cm), on all four sides. Make a cut on each side of about 1 inch (3 cm) deep. This means you will have a square base of about 2⅜ inches (6 cm). Remove all the extra wood on the sides of the base. That is easy, thanks to the cuts you made (**Figure 31**).

The result is a piece of wood that can be held firmly in the vise, from start to finish.

Figure 31. The base is a square of 6 cm by 3.5 cm high (2⅜ x 1½ inches).

**Tip:** At what height should your piece of wood be when you are carving? For a three dimensional piece, it should be at the height of your breast. If the workbench is too low, you're standing stooped over and you get a sore back. Make sure you have enough room to put your feet firmly on the ground. You must also be able to move the workpiece and/or change its position according to your needs.

Chapter 9

# Step by step to a loudly laughing face

# 1. Making a cylinder with space for a nose

Draw the plan of the head as seen from above on the top of the piece. Cut out the drawing you made, put it on top, hold it firmly and draw around it. Do not secure your drawing by pinning it in the middle onto the wood. A little hole will remain on top of the spherical head. The middle is the highest point and no wood will be removed on that spot, so any mark you put there will remain. If you do want to secure your drawing on the wood, pin it on the sides where wood will be removed, or use tape (**Figure 32** and **Figure 33**).

Now, draw a central line starting on the top and coming down on the side where the face will be (**Figure 34**).

Remove all of the wood on the outside of the drawing. Remove the corners first. Use a large hollow gouge, for example a Pfeil 8/16 to 20 mm. You can also proceed with a flatter gouge, for example a Pfeil 3/20 mm.

Do not cut away your central line. The line is the highest point of the circle. If you remove it, you damage the round shape and you have to make the whole sphere smaller. Be sure to cut with the grain. The grain runs from top to bottom. If the grain turns, you can cut across the grain.

Remove wood on both sides of the nose using a U-tool, for example, one

*Figure 32. Do not pin the plan in the middle of the wood.*

*Figure 33. Draw a circle on all four sides.*

*Figure 34. A central line starts on top and comes down on all sides.*

*Figure 35. This is the central line plus space for the nose. Remove all of the wood outside these lines.*

that is 11/7 millimeters (or even larger, up to 11/15) (**Figure 35**).

Frequently stop carving and take your piece in hand. Turn it and look at it from all angles and sides. Take your time. Look at what you've done and what remains to be done. Look at the carving from the top but also from the bottom. Forget the base for a moment and see if you have achieved a beautiful round circle. The result should be a cylinder with extra space for the nose (**Figure 36**).

 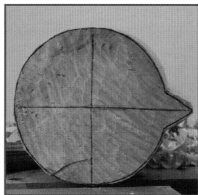

*Figure 36. A cylinder with a nose.*

# 2. Making the cylinder into a sphere

First mark the bottom of the nose. Draw a line and remove all of the wood under the line. Always use a U-tool for this. You must be very careful not to cut too deeply (**Figure 37**).

Now we can give the nose more form. The upper part of the nose can be sloped back, like a real nose. Cut away the top with an almost flat, broad gouge (3/20 or 2/20) so that you get a nice triangle that almost looks like a nose. If you look on top, the circle now looks closed again (**Figure 38** and **Figure 39**).

Next mark the center of your circle on the top, and three sides with an X or a small dot. Do not mark on the face-side. The X, or dots, are the highest points on the carving. They must stay, do not cut them away. Should that happen, replace them immediately.

With the X in place, you are ready to make the whole piece spherical. Start removing wood on the corners. Work your way up from each X to the central point on the top. This allows you to cut with the grain and avoid end grain as much as possible. At the bottom you can only take wood off until the base gets in the way (**Figure 40**).

*Figure 37. Use a U-gouge for the bottom of the nose.*

*Figure 38. On top the circle looks closed again.*

*Figure 39. Here is the first step toward a profile.*

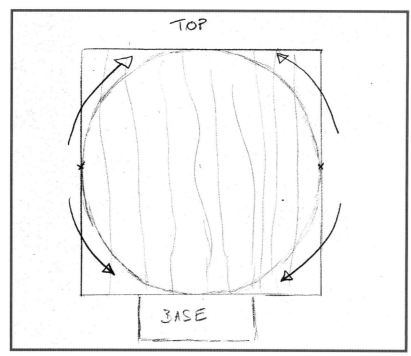

Figure 40. Carve from the central x toward the top and the bottom.

Figure 41. A sphere with a nose.

The side of the face also needs to be rounded as much as possible. Don't consider the forehead as a human forehead. In this spherical head the forehead is a part of the sphere, and doesn't really relate to a real forehead.

Now check the nose with your drawing. If the nose is too big, make it smaller. The more wood you have above the nose, the easier it is for you to make your sculpture into a sphere.

At the bottom, under the nose, also make the face-side spherical, until the base hinders you.

Do not underestimate the difficulty of making a real sphere. Here is a tip, when you cut away corners there is a flat space remaining on top. Make this flat space always round. Remember that the more wood you remove the smaller the circle will become. Always keep the central point in the middle. Do not attempt to round one side completely while neglecting the other sides. You have to work at all sides at the same time, top and bottom.

Frequently take a look at what you are doing. Take the sculpture in your hand and turn it around, and look at it from all sides. Mark the spots that need to be cut away.

The only spots where no wood has to be removed are the central points (X) on the three sides and the center point on top. If the base hinders you too much, take off the corners, so you have more room for rounding the sculpture (**Figure 41**).

# 3 The nose

When your piece is nice and round you can begin carving the face. Take the drawing of the front view of the face. Redraw the central line (is the nose still in the middle of your carving?) and draw the nose and two brow lines. Since your piece is not flat anymore, you cannot just copy the drawing.

Measure the distance of the eyebrows from the top and the distance between the eyebrows. Also measure the width of the nose in the smallest and widest place. With the help of these measured points draw the line from the eyebrow to the bottom of the nose (**Figure 42**).

Do not pin the drawing on the nose, the highest point. You will get stuck with a little hole in the nose of your carving. Use your eyes and work symmetrically. Use a pencil for drawing and keep an eraser nearby. Look at what you have drawn. Is it symmetrical? If not, try again. Only start carving when the lines you have drawn are to your satisfaction.

Carve with an 11/5-gouge along the nose line, from the bottom of the nose to the point where your grain changes direction. This is also the deepest point, the corner side of the eye near the nose. Next you need to come down with the 11/5 along the brow line. Start in the middle of the brow line (**Figure 43**).

Repeat this a couple of times and you soon develop a nose bridge. Remove the wood on the cheeks so that the nose connects with the cheeks. The sides of the nose slope

*Figure 42. The nose and brow lines are now drawn in.*

*Figure 43. Begin to develop the nose bridge.*

Figure 44. Cut in the nosewings.

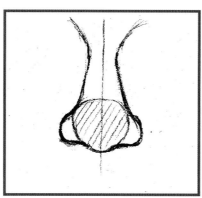

Figure 45. The high point of the nose.

down to the cheeks. Now remove the corners of the nose with a 3/16 or 2/16.

Now work on the bottom of the nose (**Figure 45**). Note that the highest point of a nose is not completely at the bottom. Remove wood from the highest point, down to the philtrum and upper part of the mouth. Do not carve the nostrils yet. First you need to work on the wings of the nose.

The spot where a nose wing touches the cheek is also the place where the nasolabial furrow starts.

The bottom of the nose is broad because when you laugh the nose broadens. The edges of your laughing mouth pull the skin away and both sides of the nose follow that movement. The nose wings are being pulled away and a little bit upward. I advise you to check it out in front of a mirror. Go from a serious look to a broad smile and keep looking at your nose wings.

Draw the nose wings. From the nose wing down draw the nasolabial furrow (**Figure 44**).

Part the nose wing from the cheek with a gouge that matches the form exactly. Here I can use a 7/10 or 7/6. Cut in and take away wood from the cheeks. By doing this you also start to create the nasolabial furrow. The furrow begins just above the nose-wing.

To form the upper part of the nose wing use a small U-gouge, a 9/2, 9/3 or 11/3 or 11/4. The nose above the wings becomes narrower, and the wings must be rounded.

# 4. Carving the nasolabial furrow

Carving the nasolabial furrow makes it possible to develop the mouth separately from the cheeks. The cheek has to become round and is pulled upward when laughing. The highest point of the cheek is closer to the eye than in a serious looking face.

The mouth is much more convex than we usually imagine. Think of those plaster models that dentists make of teeth. A mouth is placed around these teeth. The form can be compared to the letter U. The convex part is what we see when someone laughs loudly.

Draw the nasolabial furrow. Find the matching gouge (3/16 or 2/16) and cut the furrow in (**Figure 46** and **Figure 47**). Remove wood on the mouth-side. You develop the round form of the mouth by dropping the corners of the mouth. Cut the furrow in again and again, so you can make the corners of the mouth drop deep enough to make the right convex form. On the other side of the furrow lies the cheek. The wood on that side needs to be rounded for the bulging cheek (**Figure 48**).

Working on the furrow means you are carving three things at the same time, the global round form of the mouth, the roundness of the cheek and also the bottom of the nose wings and nostrils. When you take away wood to get to the right form of the mouth, you can finish the nose wings. They need to be undercut on the sides, where the furrow starts.

*Figure 46. Developing the nasolabial furrow.*

*Figure 47. A close-up of the nasolabial furrow.*

*Figure 48. One of the best ways to know if the global form of the mouth is okay, is to look at it from the bottom, upward.*

*Figure 49. The nosewings are hidden in the furrow.*

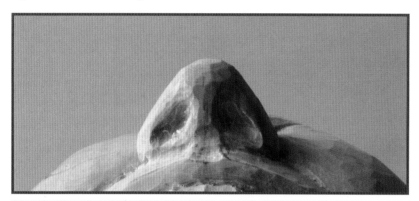

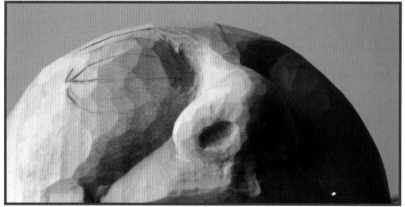

*Figure 50. We are now developing the nostrils and nose.*

At this point you can also carve the nostrils. It is also possible to wait a little longer, as you might still be altering the form of the space above the mouth. Make sure you are quite satisfied with the shape of the space above the mouth before cutting in the nostrils.

Now take another look at the profile of your piece. Is the wing of the nose higher than the bottom of the nose? The answer has to be "yes." Is the highest point of the nose at the bottom? Here the answer has to be "no." At this point you still have enough wood to make some significant changes. You should not be able to see the deepest point of the wing of the nose in profile. It is hidden behind the nasolabial furrow (**Figure 49**).

Take a small U-gouge for the nostrils, like an 11/3 or 11/4 (alternatives: 9/2, 9/3). Cut in from the sides to the middle and make the beginning of a hole. The nostril doesn't need to be very deep at the moment, just enough to make it seem like a nostril-hole. Round the sides of the nostril and make them join with the nose (**Figure 50**).

# 5. Carving the mouth and teeth

The nasolabial furrow develops into the line that goes down to the chin. It starts as a deep furrow, because the face is laughing. Down towards the chin the furrow softens. Most people have more laughing furrows, parallel to this one. But at the moment it is too soon to carve those.

It is time to start with the mouth itself. Both lips are stretched when laughing. The usual form of the lips is altered, and in fact laughing lips are easier to carve (**Figure 51**).

Draw the mouth on your carving (**Figure 52**). Find the gouge matching the bottom line of the upper lip (2/25) and make a cut on the line. Remove wood under the upper lip. Not too much, don't forget you need wood for the teeth.

Round the upper lip with a number 2 gouge, used upside down, until you reach the line you drew for the top of the lip. Also carve the philtrum (**Figure 53**). Not too deep, it is also pulled away and almost not visible. I do carve it in, slightly. Remove a bit of wood on the left and right of the philtrum.

Make a place for the upper teeth. Draw the space you need for the teeth, but do not draw them in detail. Remove the wood under and on both sides of the teeth until you reach the top of the bottom lip. Do not yet round the bottom lip, because you will damage it working on the teeth and hollowing out the mouth. Leave some superfluous wood (**Figure 54**).

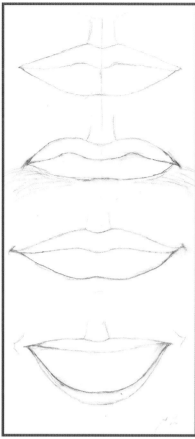

Figure 51. In a loudly laughing mouth the lips are much smaller than in a softly smiling mouth, a sad mouth, or an ordinary mouth without any expression.

Figure 52. A laughing mouth is very wide.

Figure 53. Cut in the bottom of the upper lip and carve the philtrum.

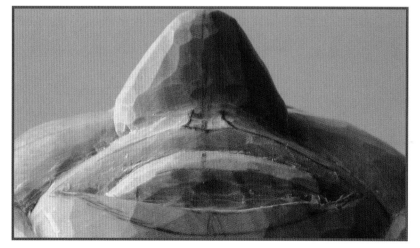

Figure 54. The teeth can be an interesting challenge. The left side is OK, the right is not deep enough.

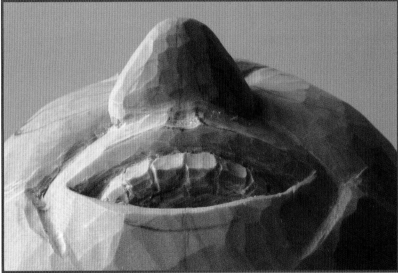

Figure 55. Cutting in the corners of the mouth also helps you to give the teeth the right round shape.

The louder you laugh, the more teeth and gums you see. I choose not to carve the lower teeth. Sometimes too much detail spoils the overall impression.

The upper lip must be undercut. You can do this while working on the teeth. You can use a small V-tool, a 15/3, but only when it is sharp. You are cutting across the grain, and a blunt tool will tear the fibers and damage the lip. Give the teeth their global round form; think back to the dentist's plaster teeth. The mouth cavity needs depth. You can create the impression of depth by cutting in deep at the corners of the mouth cavity on the left and right side of the teeth (**Figure 55**).

Now take your pencil and draw the placement of each tooth. Start with the two front teeth, one left and one right of your central line and move on. Replace your central line if you have accidentally removed it. Draw six teeth. More teeth will follow automatically when you work in the corners of the mouth.

I prefer not to give too much detail to the teeth. Very exact and detailed teeth may give the impression the teeth are unreal.

Normally a tooth is rounder towards the edges. But instead of rounding them, I take a 7/6 and make each tooth hollow, cut with some nonchalance. Look from a distance, you won't see the difference between round and hollow. Hollow is easier to cut and less work. Separate the teeth at the bottom by cutting away tiny triangles between them. Then make sure the bottom of each tooth is not too straight. Part the teeth with a narrow cut. Again, not too detailed (**Figure 56**).

Take a step backwards and look from a distance to see what impression you get.

After finishing the front of the teeth you may begin the process of undercutting. Undercutting the teeth can be a bit difficult. Try not to damage the lower lip. You can use a small gouge 11/1 or 11/2 to remove wood in the corners of the mouth. You can also carve with small gouges such as 2/3 or 3/2 or 1/2.

Leave the teeth thicker than normal to keep them strong (**Figure 57**).

Next you can begin work on the bottom lip. The bottom lip is placed around the lower teeth. You can imagine the teeth underneath the lip, which is being pulled along these teeth. Once again, think back to the dentist's plaster teeth.

Draw a line along the bottom lip, but lower, on the spot where the mouth joins the chin. This is about ½ inch (5 cm) under the lip. Cut the line in with a U-gouge, for example an 11/4 (**Figure 58**). This line marks the spot where the mouth turns into the chin.

Under the lower lip cut in again with a very hollow gouge (11/4) and begin to form the chin (**Figure 59**).

You will not be able to develop a realistic chin in a spherical head, but you do need those lines to finish the mouth. Make the lowest point of the mouth join the deepest cut. The lip needs to be

*Figure 56. Part the teeth with a narrow cut.*

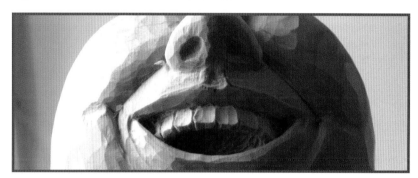

*Figure 57. The teeth are undercut but left fairly thick. A small cut at each corner of the mouth allows you to drop the lower lip.*

*Figure 58. Cut in the bottom of the mouth. This is where the mouth begins to turn into the chin.*

Figure 59. Cut in the chin.

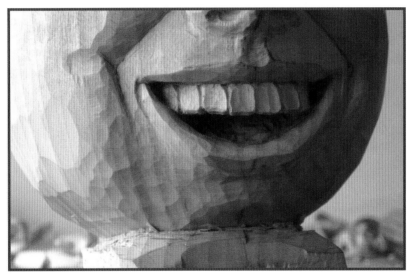

Figure 60. Use the space to round the bottom of the mouth even more.

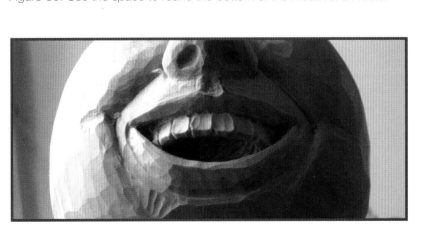

Figure 61. The bottom lip lies a bit deeper than the upper lip.

one nice round form, joining the chin and planes left and right in between the offshoot of the furrow, or between the lines coming down from the furrow (**Figure 60**).

For the left and right side of the bottom lip, start working in the corners of the mouth. The bottom lip joins the upper lip in the corner, but lies a bit deeper. Use a small, very hollow, gouge (9/2 or 11/2) to cut in at each corner. Lower the bottom lip slightly at the corner, so it joins the upper lip on a lower level (**Figure 61**).

Look often in profile, the corners of the mouth have to lie deep enough. Otherwise you cannot let the bottom lip slope backward into the corners.

Make the bottom of the sphere nicely round, with a hint at a little chin. To make your carving life easier, remove some more wood from the base at the side of the face. Make the chin part of the sphere.

# 6. Carving the cheeks and eyes

A laughing person has round, chubby cheeks. The chubbiness of a loudly laughing cheek is closer to the eye than when you are just mildly smiling, or looking serious (**Figure 62**).

The cheek pushes the bottom eyelid higher, over the eye. This means the eyes become smaller, you only see an eye slit.

We have to give the eyeball shape. But the whole eyeball is still too high; it needs to be brought down. Draw the eyeball on the sculpture, the eye fits in it. Drop the eyeball by cutting in around it.

Near the nose work with a U-gouge (11/4) and carve the line of the eyeball. Come down from the eyebrow to the nose and from the bottom of the eyeball cut upward to the nose. Use a flat gouge 3/8 or 2/8 to further shape and round the eyeball (**Figure 63**).

Start to lower the eyeball. One side is already round thanks to the spherical shape of the sculpture.

The line under the eyes, near the cheekbone, marks the spot where the cheek is pushed towards the eye when you are laughing. This is the line to cut in when you work on the outer side of the eyeball (**Figure 62**).

Repeat cutting in these lines to lower the eyeball.

When you work on the shape of

*Figure 62. There is not much space between the eyelid and the laughing cheek. Cut in on this line.*

*Figure 63. Lower and round the eyeball.*

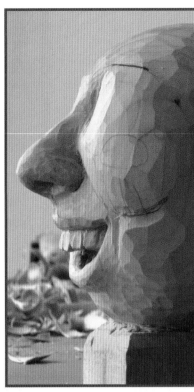

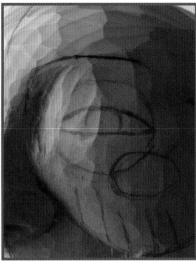

the eyeball you are shaping also the muscle that comes down from the nose to the cheek (**Figure 64**).

Do not forget to make the cheek very round just under the eyeball, at the corner of the eye. Work on it while you lower the eyeball. This is done by cutting in the lines around the eyeball with the 11/4 (**Figure 65**).

*Figure 64. The small circles show the highest points of a laughing cheek. The hatched part needs to be lowered towards the bottom of the cheek.*

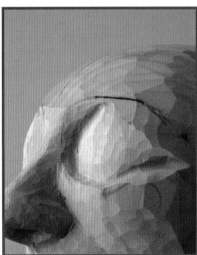

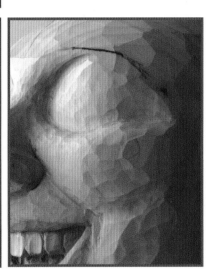

*Figure 65. The lowered eyeball and top of the cheek.*

# 7. The eyes in detail

Take your pencil and redraw the eyes when you are satisfied with the round shape of the eyeball (**Figure 66**).

Now draw the lower eyelid. It is very thick, and when you draw it you'll notice that the eye now looks a lot more like a full, complete eye. The lower eyelid covers the lower part of the eye because you are laughing (**Figure 67**).

You can carve the eye now. Find the gouges matching the shape of the eye. Here a 3/8 and 2/5 can be used, and an 11/2 (or 9/2) for the little hole in the corner of the eye (**Figure 68**).

The eye has to be lowered about $\frac{1}{16}$ inch (1 to 1.5 millimeters). Drop the corners, especially the corner near the nose. Do not make the upper and lower sides too round! Think of the complete eyeball, it disappears under the flesh, you need to make the eye look like only a part of a sphere. The left and right corners go much deeper than the bottom and upper side.

The lower eyelid needs to be very full, cut in with a really small U-gouge, a small 11 or a small 9, under the line you drew. The cut has to be extremely close to the cheek. You need to make a connection from the lower eyelid to the top of the cheek, on the outside of the eye.

For the upper eyelid you can draw a line parallel to the shape of the eye. Again, with gouges matching

*Figure 66. Redraw the eye slit on the sphere.*

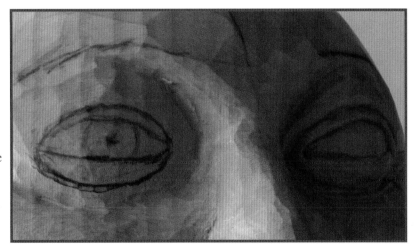
*Figure 67. The eye and eyelids.*

*Figure 68. The eye cut in.*

*Figure 69. The eye with upper and lower eyelids.*

*Figure 70. The eye cover fold slopes backwards.*

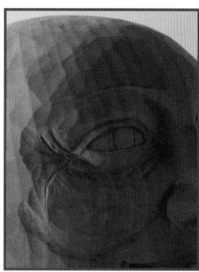

*Figure 71. The laugh wrinkles and the iris are drawn on the eye.*

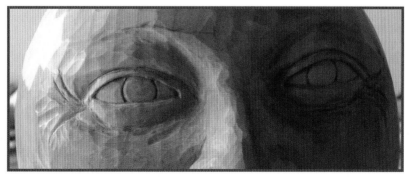

*Figure 72. The iris is cut and the edges are slightly rounded.*

the shape, cut in the line. The upper eyelid needs to slope upward. Your gouge should be inclined when you cut in the eyelid, remember there's a ball underneath, follow the slope of the eyeball. Then round the eye cover fold but do not take away too much wood. Round the wood to the deepest point of the upper eyelid.

On the outside of the eye the lower eyelid folds under the upper eyelid (**Figure 69**).

The eye cover fold is not realistic. The sphere slopes backwards too much for a normal eye cover fold (**Figure 70**).

Laugh wrinkles are very important for the laughing face. These deep wrinkles appear at the sides of the eye and top of the cheek. Sketch these lines in. They start at the outside of the eye. Some go upward, others downward on the edge of the cheek. You need to cut them in, and round the sides of the deep laugh wrinkles. You cannot work with a U-gouge or a V-tool because you will lose too much wood (**Figure 71**).

Draw the iris in, and find the matching gouge to cut in the line. I do not hollow out the iris in this sculpture. I do not want to make the eyes too striking. I round the edges a bit, that is all (**Figure 72**).

# 8. Finishing the furrows around the mouth

Now you still have to cut the furrows that run from the nasolabial furrow down to the chin, or parallel with them. Some people also have a little laughing hole just under the cheek. Draw in the furrows, the little hole is optional.

I also decided to alter the nasolabial furrows. I will take them a little bit closer to the cheek; this also pushes the cheek upwards. (**Figure** 73).

*Figure 73. Nasolabial furrows around the mouth go down to the chin. The cheeks are now a bit higher.*

*Figure 74. Leave a tiny base if you want to grip your carving in a vise for sanding.*

# 9. Tidying up and removing the base

Do this by daylight, in the morning, when you are not tired.

The features of the laughing face are all carved in. The only thing left to do is to tidy the carving with a gouge before you can start sanding.

Have a final look at the form of your sphere. Take a large almost flat gouge, 2/25 or 2/30. Improve the shape and remove any ugly cuts. Also tidy any bad cuts in the face.

Tidying the surface is very important. Sanding a blemish away takes much longer than cutting it away! If you take your time here, you will not have to spend as much time sanding. Believe me, carving is much more fun than sanding!

The chin must be rounded if it is too protruding.

The base has to be removed. You can take it off completely, or leave a very small base, not strong enough for carving, but strong enough to put your carving in the vise for sanding. Afterward you can remove the remaining tiny base (**Figure 74**).

To remove the base use a large gouge, a number 2, and a U-tool, 11, with your mallet. Cut in, following the shape of the sphere and remove wood from the base. Make it smaller by repeating until you remove it completely. The idea is to make the lower part of the sphere round. This will probably take more time than you expect. You still have to shape

**Tip:** Take frequent pictures of your work. Afterward it is wonderful to show your friends and to see for yourself the progress you have made. If you want to have some nice photos of your carvings, make sure you get a good close-up. Choose a neutral background, a white sheet or a black cloth for example. Try to get your carving sharp and the background hazy.

quite a lot of the sphere on the bottom. You are not just removing the base.

When you are almost there, don't break off the small remaining base. Doing that would damage the wood fibers, leaving little holes of broken wood fibers in the bottom.

If you saw the base off, there is a chance the bottom will be too flat and the shape of the sphere damaged. Furthermore, it will leave you with an ugly uncarved spot and the sphere will not be able to be gripped firmly any more in a vise. You will damage the wood, especially softwood such as linden/lime, if you try to put it in the vise. Even if you wrap the sphere in a piece of thick cloth or leather, the vise can easily damage it. Do not attempt to keep the sphere in your hand while working on it with a carving tool. It is much too dangerous (**Figure 75**).

Is the sphere a beautiful sphere? Are most of the tool marks cut away? You are now ready to start sanding your carving.

*Figure 75. The base is removed.*

Chapter 10

# Sanding your carving

I sand most of my carvings. I sand because I want to draw the attention to the lines of the wood, to the beautiful grain. Gouge cuts usually make other lines less conspicuous.

If the piece is not too big I do the sanding by hand. You could use a machine for sanding, but only for the sphere, not for the face. Even then you have to do the final sanding of the sphere by hand.

Begin sanding only when you have a surface with a minimum of tool marks. Although there may be few tool marks you will spend quite some time sanding. It always feels like it will never end. Take a regular break to spare your fingertips. Gloves can help, but I find it too difficult to work accurately with them. I prefer no gloves and more breaks for coffee or tea.

Sanding does not mean you must sand everything away. On the contrary, you need to preserve the character of your carving. It is very possible to make a beautiful carving and sand it into a dull, uninteresting piece of work. Keep this in mind when you start sanding. Do not sand away the beautiful facial details.

Use good quality sanding materials. I prefer to work with sanding strips of cloth. You can use aluminum oxide sandpaper or garnet paper.

Sandpaper is defined by grit. It is a reference to the number of abrasive particles per inch of sandpaper. The smaller the grit number, the rougher the sandpaper. A 40 grit to 60 grit paper is very coarse and is used for heavy sanding. The 80 to 120 grit is used to remove the smaller marks

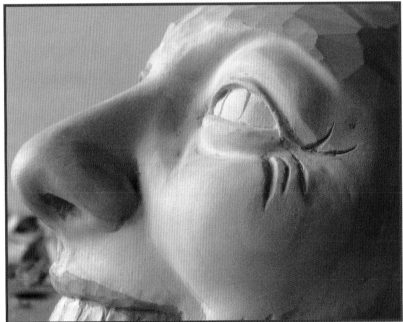

Figure 76. Sanding will reshape the facial features.

*Figure 77. After sanding with 320 grit paper the face looks rather dull and lifeless.*

and imperfections. I work through the very fine grits 220 and 240. My final grit is extra fine, 280 to 320.

For limewood (Tilia spp, also called linden and basswood) I start with 100 grit for the face. Limewood is rather soft and you can damage the fibers with a coarse sandpaper such as 60 grit. You can start with 80 grit for the rest of the sphere. For sanding a sphere you cannot wrap sandpaper around a block. That method is good for flat surfaces, not for round ones.

Remember you must go through all the grits, from coarse to fine. Do not go to a finer grit if you still have blemishes! Each progressive piece of sandpaper removes the scratches from the previous sandpaper. If you skip a grit to save time you will often end up sanding longer just to remove the scratches left by the previous grit.

When you see a fault at the final stage go back to a coarser sandpaper, sand the problem away, go through all the grits again, and only then finish with 320 grit.

For sanding, as well as for carving, you need good light, and I really prefer to do it in daylight. Artificial lighting can cause shadows that give you a wrong impression.

As you are finishing your carving I'm sure you don't want to spoil all your work, so make sure you are not in a hurry, and not tired.

Sanding the face means re-shaping the face. You need to bear in mind the anatomy of a face, and each detail in it. It is like carving, but with a different tool. The dust makes the process of sanding more difficult because it takes away depth, color, and overview.

Do not blow the dust away because you are liable to blow it into your face and eyes. You can use a brush or cloth to carefully wipe the dust away. If you do this regularly, it is easier to see where you still have to sand.

Be careful if you work with tropical woods. The dust is often poisonous. Using a dust-mask is always a good idea, but a necessity for some tropical woods. Don't take any risks, you can be allergic to the dust without knowing it.

Fold the sandpaper when working in the furrows, for example when working under the eye or between the eye and cheek. Look often to see that there are still abrasive particles in the fold. If not, refold your sandpaper.

For a shallow curve, roll the paper into a small cylinder that fits the shape of the contour. I always use small pieces of sandpaper that allow me to work with accuracy on the right spot. A large piece can damage the surrounding wood.

When sanding the eyeball be very careful not damage the eyelids (**Figure 76**).

After the sanding your carving may look rather dull, colorless and without depth (**Figure 77**).

It is best if you can carve in some details again, such as the upper eyelid, the laughing-wrinkles, (**Figure 78**) and the eyeball where it disappears under the eyelids.

I usually do not sand the lips and teeth, or the inside of the mouth.

*Figure 78. After sanding, the sharp details need to be finished with a gouge cut.*

Chapter 11

# Finishing

*Figure 79. At the first brush stroke the carving comes alive.*

There are many ways to finish a carving. The most important question is what you want to achieve. What do you like? Do you want to enhance the grain of the wood? Do you want to keep the natural color of the wood? Do you want a glossy finish? A satin finish?

You can test different finishes on another piece of sanded wood to see the effect of your finish.

I want my carvings to be appealing to people. I am glad if they want to touch my carvings, feel them, and smell them. I want a soft finish, not too shiny and a good smell. I prefer a natural look, I like to see all the beautiful lines of the wood. I never stain my pieces. That is why I usually choose an oil finish. The oil enhances the figure of the wood and it is a very natural finish.

Linseed oil is well known and traditionally used as a finish for carvings. I do not like it and have never really used it. You can find linseed oil either raw or boiled. The raw linseed oil takes a long time to dry, up to three days. Boiled linseed oil takes about 24 hours to dry.

I often use tung oil, a very durable oil finish. It is oil made from the fruit of the Chinese tung

*Figure 80. One coat of tung oil plus orange oil.*

tree (*Aleurites fordii*) and thus sometimes called China wood oil. It is very durable and also water resistant. Drying time is usually about 24 hours per coat.

If you are looking for a matte oil finish, lemon oil is an excellent choice. It is made from lemongrass oil and is also water-resistant. It has a nice, fresh smell. Give your carving 24 hours to dry between each coat.

Recently I have started to use orange oil. It is a perfect oil to mix with tung oil (or linseed oil). It is a very natural product and it smells like you've just opened a bottle of sweet, fruity perfume.

I mix it with Chinese tung oil (70% tung oil, 30% orange oil). The brand I use is an ecological product that has no added dryers. I apply the oil with a brush or a cloth and let it soak into the wood for a couple of minutes. Then I remove any excess oil with a clean cloth or paper towel. I give it enough time to dry after each coat. I give a carving a minimum of four coats and as many as six (**Figure 79, Figure 80, Figure 81**).

I also use Danish oil, a commercially prepared finish similar to tung oil, with siccatives added. This means your carving dries quickly, sometimes six hours can be enough, depending on the place where you leave it to dry. Use the same application procedure as for tung oil.

Protective gloves should be worn when working with finishes. Be certain to properly dispose of any rags or other finishing materials because there is always the danger of spontaneous combustion. Spread oily rags outdoors to dry, then you can put the dried rags in the trash.

After four to six coats I want to make the wood really smooth and soft. When the last coat is completely dry, sand with a waterproof sandpaper, extremely fine, 600 grit. I put some olive oil on the sandpaper and go over the complete carving. Then I wipe it clean and dry with a cloth or paper towel. You now should have a very soft, natural looking carving.

I do not often give my carvings a wax coating. Wax can be very beautiful but it is easy to fill the details with wax, and it is absolutely necessary to avoid that. If you use too much wax the carving gets sticky and attracts dust.

*Figure 81. Two coats of tung oil plus orange oil.*

Chapter 12

# What happens in a sad face?

The emotion of sadness lies close to the emotion of disappointment, and also to anger. You can be so sad that you start crying. Note that crying is not one simple emotion. There are many ways of crying. You can cry like a child, tears just come pouring out of your eyes. You can cry out of inability, you wanted to do something, but it didn't work out. You can cry for a loss, I call that existential crying, the worst and deeply felt sadness. It is such a horrible feeling I do not want you to try to relive it when you are carving. That is not the sadness I chose for this crying wood.

In this spherical face the emotion of sadness lies close to angry sadness, crying because you want to achieve something, you wanted it very much, but you didn't get it (**Figure 82**).

The mouth is a very important sign of your feelings. A laughing mouth is big; the corners pulled up in a smile, pushing up the cheeks. For a sad, angry, face you see the opposite, the corners of the mouth go down and pull the skin around down with it.

The upper lip goes down steeply, and is narrower than usual and the corners lower than normal. The lower lip is jutted out, and thicker than usual. The projecting of this lip pulls the skin around forward and closer to the chin.

If you cry with lots of tears, you push your lip really forward, think of a crying child, it always cries with enthusiasm. The lower lip looks broader than the upper lip.

*Figure 82. A sad, and possibly a bit angry, face.*

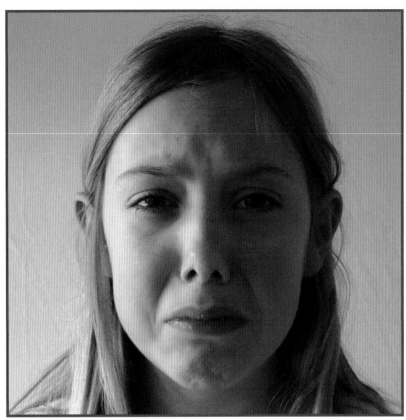

*Figure 83. She is very close to crying, but luckily, only posing.*

The nasolabial furrow is deepened, but also a little bit rounded, just at the height of the nose wings. The furrow accentuates the downward direction of the whole face.

In a laughing face everything seems to be pulled or pushed upwards. However, in a sad face it is all contrary, everything is going down.

The eyebrows are lowered and pulled closer to the eye. The lines of the eyebrows change. This causes wrinkles on the forehead, and more specifically on the spot were the nose joins the forehead. Older people already have one or two wrinkles there. These will be deepened if they cry or are sad. Young people do not have these wrinkles if they look happy or just normal. But if they look sad or cry they also get wrinkles. It is in these places that in older age the wrinkles will be developed and persist.

The eyelid is also pushed down a bit closer to the eye. If someone has been crying a long time, the whole area around the eye thickens.

You should go stand in front of the mirror and look what happens in your face when you think of something sad and would like to start crying. Try this, sit down and put your fingertips on your face. Now think of something sad, and feel what is happening in your face. Go from laughing to a normal look, and then to a sad face. Do you feel the difference? Try it several times and touch your cheeks, mouth, corners of the mouth, your chin, your eyebrows, wrinkles. And when you go to looking sad, feel on the side of your nose, you can feel a muscle from behind the wing of the nose pushing the nasolabial furrow a little bit away.

If you are carving an emotion the most important thing for you is to know what the emotion looks like. Everyone knows how it feels, but what you have to learn are the tangible effects of an emotion displayed in a face (**Figure 84**).

In this drawing the sphere is not completely round anymore. You still want to give the impression of a sphere. But if it is really round, the face will look too happy, because the roundness refers to chubby cheeks. That is why I flattened the sides slightly. Make it a subtle change, so that the cheeks don't give you the idea of happiness.

*Figure 84. A sad face.*

Chapter 13

# Make a drawing

For a sad face you need some plans and drawings to help you.

First of all you need to know how big your piece of wood is. You can make a drawing as big as your wood, or you can just draw it any dimension you like and then make some photocopies in the exact dimensions.

Start with the easiest drawing, a circle.

Next make another one, but slightly flatten the sides. This will be the simple plan for your front view and back view (**Figure 85**).

Now, you can make a simple drawing of the head as seen from the top. Copy the flattened circle and draw a nose on it. Next draw a second line, a protruding piece of wood is needed for the mouth. The bottom lip is projected really far, pulling a lot of skin forward. This means you need to predict now how much extra wood you will need around the mouth (**Figure 86**).

With this sad looking face it is very helpful to have a good drawing of the profile. It will help you to realise how exactly you are going to put a face on the sphere. On the following drawing you see the nose and lower part of the mouth coming out of the sphere. The nose bridge will get deeper than the line of the sphere. With the eyebrows we come back onto the shape of the sphere (**Figure 87**).

Make a useable plan from the profile drawing (**Figure 88**).

For a front view drawing try out

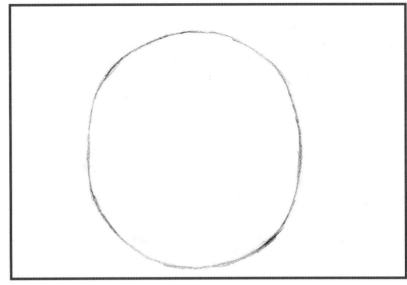

Figure 85. A basic plan for your front and back view.

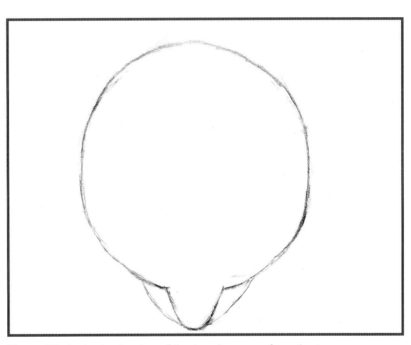

Figure 86. A simple drawing of the head as seen from the top.

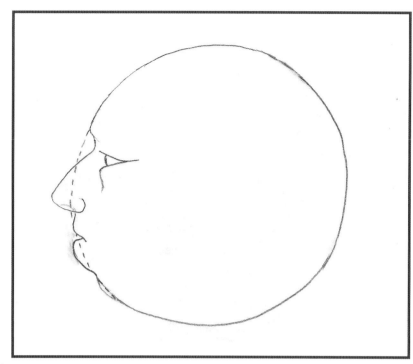

*Figure 87. The profile.*

your knowledge of sadness in a face. First copy the flattened circle. Draw a central line to help you draw and work symmetrically. Draw a nose to start. Then a very important line in a sad face, the nasolabial furrow. This furrow is found around the nose wing and in this case is slightly rounder than normal. The upper lip will be rather small and curved down, as will the corners of the mouth. The bottom lip is thick, heavy and protruding. The eyes are not too large and the eyebrows come down to the nose, and are lowered (**Figure 89**).

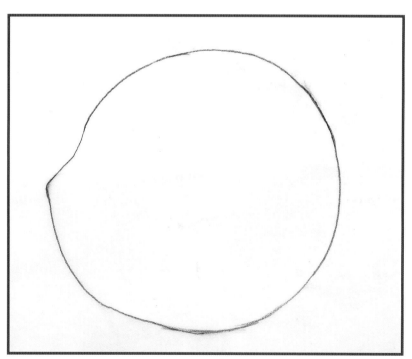

*Figure 88. A useable profile plan to put on the wood.*

Figure 89. The front view.

Chapter 14

# Step by step to sadness

# 1. Choose and prepare your wood

I will carve the sad face in a piece of pearwood. It has been lying around my workshop for a while and is very dry. There are cracks in it. I feel the cracks in the wood and sadness go very well together. The color is red-brown. Compared to the previous carving, in lime, this wood is darker, harder, and finer grained.

With lime I seldom use a mallet, but with pear I will certainly use one, especially for the rough work in the beginning and also for the extra fine work and details.

The piece looks rather straight at first sight, but isn't (**Figure 90**). It has no square edges. Most pieces look rather straight but aren't. You can plane the piece of wood until you have a perfectly square piece. This makes it easy to apply your drawings. If you don't have a machine, use your eyes. Draw straight lines on the wood on all four sides. Turn the piece, and make the lines meet. Then work within the straight lines, and forget the crooked edges.

The dimensions of this piece are 8 inches (21 cm) high, 4 inches (11 cm) wide and 5½ inches (13.8 cm) thick. It is much too long, but I decided to keep the length and give it an extra long base. This is better than having a base that is too short.

Remember, the sphere for this sad face is not a perfect sphere, the drawing of the front view is 4 inches

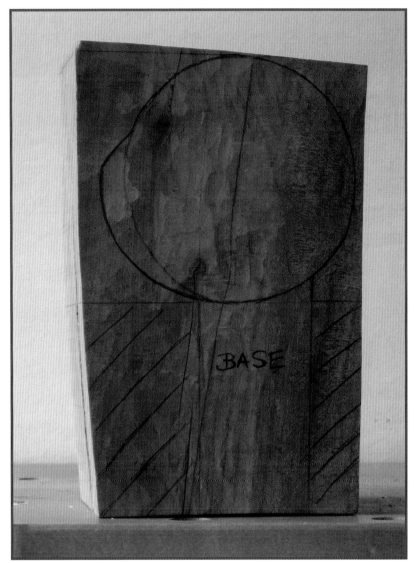

Figure 90. Pear is a hard, fine-grained wood.

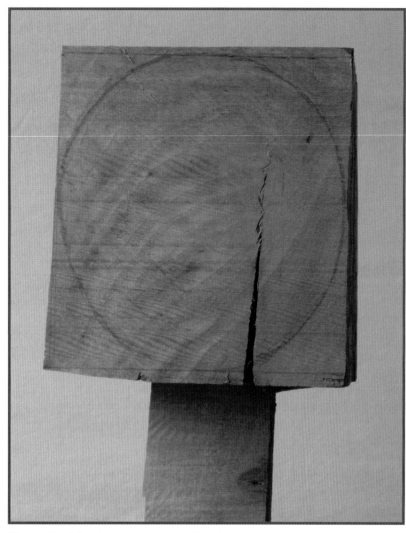

*Figure 91. A front view with the outline drawn.*

*Figure 92. Note the base is not in the middle of the sphere.*

(11 cm) wide, by 4½ inches (11.5 cm) high (**Figure 91**).

The profile drawing is a sphere of 4½ inches (11.5 cm) plus the extra space for nose and mouth. Together this means I need about 5 inches (12.3 cm) in profile. Because I have about 5½ inches (13.8 cm), a little over ½ inch (1.5 cm) will have to be removed. Draw the profile on the wood.

I did not put the base exactly in the middle, but instead I put it closer to the back. Thus I get more free room to work on the face later on. The base will be a square of 2 inches (5 cm). This is smaller than for the limewood carving, but the pear is really strong wood and a base of 5 centimeters is quite enough. The smaller you can make to base, the better: you have more space to shape the sphere and face (**Figure 92**).

2. Make a cylinder with space for a nose and mouth

With a piece of wood that has no straight edges you need to be very careful to make a good and correct start. Draw straight lines on your wood so that you can visualize a piece with straight lines and edges. Each line needs to join another one at every edge.

All plans need to be drawn inside the straight lines.

Place an X on top of your carving, in the middle. Do the same on three sides but not on the face side. The X's are the highest points of the sphere.

Draw the plan of the spherical head, as seen from the top, on your piece of wood. Remove all of the wood outside of the plan. I use a large gouge and mallet, a number 7 or 8, minimum ¾ inch (20 mm) broad. Next I remove the deep gouge cuts with a large number 2, up to 1¼ inches (35 mm).

While I was working on the wood, I noticed that the cracks in the side of the face were too deep. At this early stage you still have plenty of wood to solve problems. So, I decided to turn the plan around. The face will come at what was going to be the back of the head. The side that was to be the face will now become the back of the head. Draw the plan of the head again on the top of the wood, removing the lines of the old plan. Do not forget to erase the old lines as they can be confusing.

Now my base was too close to the face. I took off another centimeter, to give me enough space to work on the face.

Having taken off all the wood outside your plan, you now have a cylinder with extra wood for the nose and mouth (**Figure 93**).

*Figure 93. The first step is to remove all of the wood outside of the drawing as seen from the top.*

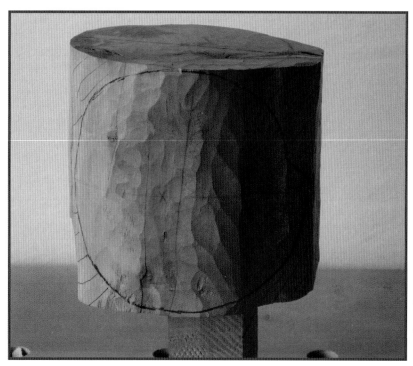

Figure 94. The profile.

# 3. Make the cylinder into a sphere

Draw the profile plan on your carving (**Figure 94**). Do not push the plan down on the cylinder you have created. This will make your plan smaller and the lines you copy will not be correct. Hold the plan in the middle (do not stick a pin in the middle, because the little hole will not be cut away) and try to draw lines around it. Take your plan away and look at what you have drawn. You might need to correct it visually. Measure the diameter to be certain your circle is large enough.

Now remove all of the wood outside of your profile plan (**Figure 95**).

Next mark the space for the nose and mouth on the face side of your carving (**Figure 96** and **Figure 97**).

This part needs to remain like it is now, while you start rounding the rest of the sphere. Take your time in carving the sphere. The X's help you to see where the middle of your circle is. You will need to remove wood everywhere, except for the spot where an X is, and the space for the nose and mouth. Make sure not to leave ugly tool marks on the sides of the space for the mouth and nose. This extra wood has to join the rest of the sphere without making deep cuts in the wood. Always use a very hollow gouge to make the sides of the nose area join the cheeks. Gouge numbers 8 to 11 will do.

Figure 95. The profile showing more wood removed.

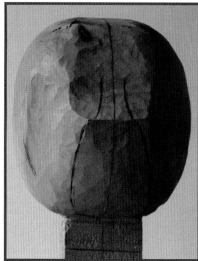

Figure 96. The space for the nose and mouth are marked out.

Carve with the grain, otherwise you might loosen big chunks of wood where you need them (**Figure 97, Figure 98, Figure 99**).

With the sphere finished, and the space for the nose and mouth ready on the face side, you can now start carving the sad face. Is your central line still there? If not, start by redrawing it.

*Figure 98. A bit of definition along the sides of the nose.*

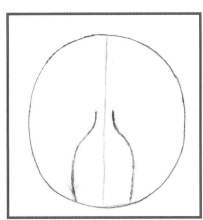

*Figure 97. Space for nose and mouth.*

*Figure 99. The sphere in profile.*

Figure 100. Front view.

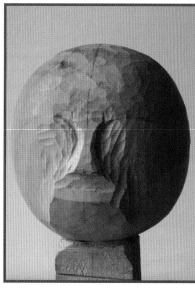

Figure 101. Draw the nose and eyebrow lines and cut along the nose area.

Figure 102. Develop a nose bridge. The nose bridge comes below the outline of the sphere.

# 4. Getting started with the nose

Use the drawing of the front view, **Figure 100**, and draw the nose and eyebrow lines on your carving.

Remove the excess wood outside the nose line. There will be too much wood for the nose and mouth area. Too much wood is no problem. It allows you to be able to change or adapt your design, if necessary. Too much wood can be cut away, but not enough wood means you will have to make the whole face and sphere smaller.

Cut in the sides of the nose with a very hollow gouge, 11/5. Go along the nose line, from the bottom of the nose to the point where your grain changes direction. This is also the deepest point, the corner side of the eye near the nose. Next you need to come down with the number 11/5 along the brow line. Start in the middle of the brow line (**Figure 101**).

Repeat this a couple of times until you develop a nose bridge, but the deepest point of the nose bridge must cave into the sphere.

Put your profile drawing nearby. It is very difficult to draw it on the wood, but make sure to look at it often. You will see that:

-the deepest point of the nose is almost ¼ inch (6 mm) deeper than the outline of the sphere;

-the bottom of the nose is about $\frac{1}{16}$ inch (1.5mm to 2 mm) below the sphere;

-the upper lip protrudes about ¾ inch (1.5mm to 2 mm);

-the lower lip bulges about ¼ inch (6 mm) outside the sphere. The bulging area around the lower lip is the main reason for our big chunk of extra wood here.

Remove wood on the cheeks. The cheek is a strong ¾ inch (2 cm) lower than the highest point of the nose. The sides of the nose slope downward to the cheeks.

Lower the nose bridge ¼ inch (6mm to 7 mm). To achieve this depth, you need to repeat several cuts. Lower the nose bridge with a very hollow gouge. Carve along the line you drew for the nose with the 11/5 and come down from the eyebrows. Lower the cheeks and eye area. Let the nose slope down to the deepest point of the nose bridge. Use an almost flat gouge, like a number 2.

Repeat this until the nose bridge is about a ¼ inch (6mm or 7 mm) under the sphere line (**Figure 102**). Every time you cut away your middle line, draw it back. It is your only reference to make the nose end up in the middle of the face. Also draw the outline of the nose again, so you can cut alongside these lines with the 11/5.

Mark the bottom of the nose and cut it in with a hollow gouge. Work carefully so that you do not damage the transition into the philtrum and mouth area.

Draw the nose wings on. The nose wings in this face are not on the same line as the bottom of the nose (the bottom is the spot that your

Figure 103. The bottom of the nose. Keep lowering the cheeks under the eyeball.

central line passes through). Look at the drawing of the front view. Take a number 3/8 gouge and cut the corners slightly higher, before you cut in the nose wings.

Part the nose wing from the cheek with a gouge that matches the form exactly. Here I can use a number 7/6 gouge. Cut in and take away wood from the cheeks.

Make the sides of the nose slope down toward the cheeks. Continue lowering the cheeks. Draw a line where the eyeball ends and the cheek starts and cut in with a very hollow gouge. Now you can lower the cheeks further and make the eye area slope down to the cheek, starting at the eyebrow line (**Figure 103**).

Take your carving in your hand and look at it in profile. Do this frequently. Does the nose bridge drop, and are the cheeks lowered enough? Also look from the bottom. You should see a protruding mouth area and a triangle for the nose. The cheek on the left must come down as far as the cheek on the right.

Now, if your carving has a nose like the one on your drawing, and has cheeks much lower, it is time for the next step.

*Figure 104. Cut in the nasolabial furrow. This allows you to work under the nose and on the mouth area.*

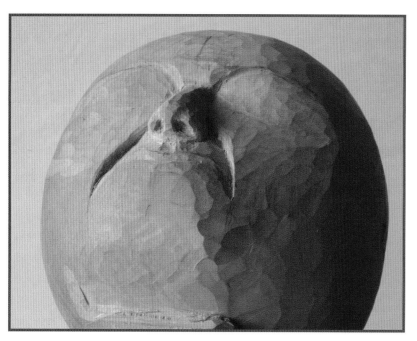

*Figure 105. The nose with the nostrils and nose wings.*

# 5. Carving the nasolabial furrow.

Carving the nasolabial furrow makes it possible in every face, whatever the emotion, to develop the mouth separately from the cheeks.

The nasolabial furrow is pulled away from your nose a little bit when you start to cry. In some faces you can even see the muscle at the height of the nose wings that pulls the furrow aside. Crying deepens the complete furrow.

Draw the nasolabial furrow. Cut in with a gouge that follows the shape of the furrow. The area within the furrow, around the nose, needs to slope down to the deepest point of the furrow. On the outside of the furrow is the cheek (**Figure 104**).

While you are working around the nose, finish the nosewings and make nostrils (**Figure 105**).

# 6. Carving the mouth

Remember drawing the lips on the laughing face (page 49)? That drawing is reproduced below as **Figure 107**.

Draw the philtrum and upper lip on your carving. The upper lip is now still a part of the high area, which we need for the protruding lower lip. This means that before you even start to shape the upper lip, you need to lower this area for the upper lip, up to the nose, by quite a lot. Look to your profile view. The upper lip is just over the outline of the sphere, the lower lip is sticking out by about ¼ inch (5 mm).

Choose a gouge that matches the lower line of the upper lip. Here a number 5/12 will do nicely. It is the exact spot where the two lips need to be parted.

Cut in and lower the upper lip and area above the mouth to the bottom of the nose (**Figure 106**).

You will need to cut in the line that parts the two lips quite often. This will make it possible to work on both lips separately.

Redraw the lips and philtrum as soon as you think the lip, and the area around it, have been lowered enough. With a very hollow gouge carve the philtrum. The philtrum looks a bit like a small triangle; the deepest cut needs to be made close to the lip. Make sure your gouge is sharp before you start. Tearing the fibers in such a small space can be catastrophic, or at least, very annoying. Also drop the wood right

Figure 106. Lower the upper lip area.

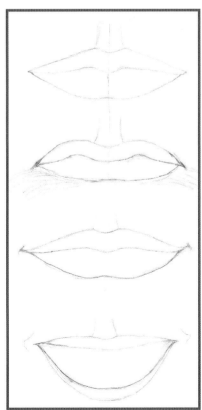

Figure 107. Drawing the mouth.

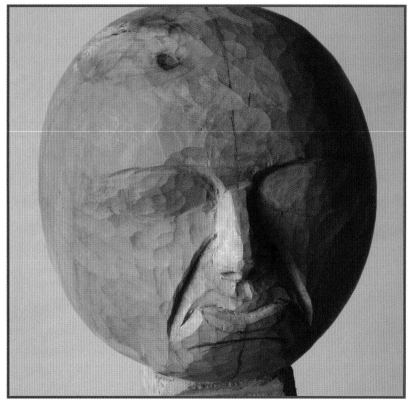

Figure 108. Note the line between lip and chin. This must be cut in with a U-gouge.

Figure 109. By cutting in several times one can lower the chin.

and left of the philtrum to form the right and left side of the philtrum.

Cut back in the line parting the two lips with the same gouge. The number 5/12 matches the line exactly. Now shape the upper lip by cutting wood away from the upper lip, at the parting line. The lip must slope inwards. You cannot take away enough wood because a big piece of wood, the lower lip, is hindering you.

Next refine the lower lip. It is sticking out and pulls the skin down and forward. Draw a line between chin and mouth, and use an 11 to part the mouth and chin (**Figure 108**). Lower the chin. Remove some wood from the chin, the lower, protruding, lip and skin comes into shape by doing this.

Now concentrate on the lower lip. The lower lip is thicker than the upper lip. The lower lip will give the impression of being broader when finished because the surrounding skin seems to make the lip longer. Make the corners of the upper lip droop, by giving the nose a downward direction. Cut in the sides of the upper lip with a very small hollow gouge (number 11/1). Then remove wood from the lower lip, rounding it toward the drooping corners. Even protruding as it is, think of the lip lying around the teeth. You need to round the lip some more, together with the skin. Do not cut the central line away, this means you take away the wood that you need to stick out, but round the wood going from this central line down to the corners of the mouth (**Figure 109**).

# 7. Carving the eyes

While working on the nose, you have already lowered the cheeks. Now you can concentrate on the eyes. Draw the eyes, and another parallel line a bit lower. You may add a tear, for a dramatic touch (**Figure 110**).

I decided not to put an iris and pupil in this crying eye. I would like to create the impression of an eye, blinded with tears. Someone who cries isn't able to see very well. I certainly do not want this face to be staring intensely by carving in a hollow pupil.

Someone who cries often has small eyes, but the tear bags are swollen. The line under the eyes needs to be cut in with a small U-gouge to form a thick tear bag. Round the tear bag to the deepest point of your cut.

The cheekbones are near the eyes. The U-cut is the spot where the eye area joins the cheekbone. Let the cheek slope towards this line (**Figure 111**).

Before you can carve the eye, you need to round the space around the eye. Think of the eyeball, the shape of a circle, under the skin. Take a hollow gouge and make a cut from the outside corner of the eye to the outside of the sphere. There is a lot of space, caused by the spherical shape. This is not realistic. Carve this line so that you can slope the eye cover fold down to it, and round off the cheekbone to this same line. Also with a U-gouge make a cut next to the inner corner of the

Figure 110. Draw the eyes and a bit lower, a parallel line. You may wish to add a tear.

Figure 111. Cut under the eye with a U-gouge. Also, using a U-gouge, cut from the outside corner of the eye to the outside of the head.

*Figure 112. One eye and tear, but the lower eyelid has yet to be carved.*

**Tip:** Periodically take a step back from your workbench. Look at your carving from a distance. Sit down and look at it from a different angle. Doing so gives you better insight and you will see new possibilities, and new solutions.

eye, near the nose. This allows you to make the eyeball round, sloping down to the lowest point.

You can carve a tear near the eye. The tear is very small. Cut in the tear, but start to round the drop as soon as possible. Otherwise, you might cut into it with the corner of a gouge, and lose a part of the tear, or the whole tear. Don't forget, the tear is placed on the eyeball, and the eyeball is round. Don't stop rounding the eyeball on the spot where the tear is. You didn't need to foresee extra wood for the teardrop, because when you round the eyeball, there is enough wood for the tear.

As soon as the eyeball is rounded, you can cut in the eye. Find the matching gouges to cut in the line of the eye (here I can use a number 5/12, and 5/3). Lower the eye and make it rounder.

The upper eyelid is partly hidden in the overhanging eye cover fold. The eye cover fold is lowered because in this crying, sad face, the eyebrow pulls the cover fold down to the eye. Do not make the upper eyelid too obvious. A small lid, not cut in too deep is enough.

The lower eyelid sits in the swollen tear bag and is small. If you make it too prominent, you lose the tear bag.

The result must be a small eye, with a large tear bag underneath, and heavy eye cover fold hanging over the eye (**Figure 112**).

# 8. Furrows and unevenness in the forehead and chin

As opposed to the smooth forehead found in a laughing face, we need unevenness for a sad, a troubled, or angry face. We need furrows from the forehead to the nose bridge.

An uneven, broad chin is also an important sign for this emotion.

In the forehead of a sad face you see a frown in the form of a triangle. Take another look at **Figure 100.** The skin on the forehead is pulled to the nose and near the top of the nose frowns and furrows come into existence. The skin also pushes the eyebrows down to the nose. You can make one or two deeper furrows from the nose to the forehead. Some people have one, others have two. The more frowns and furrows you carve, the more the expression becomes troubled.

You can start with a deep frown near the nose. Once you have carved this, you already have an idea of the impact on the face. It tells you what to do next. Does it look troubled enough? Draw some lines on the forehead, to see what effect they could make (**Figure 113**).

The chin is broader than usual and very uneven. Take a number 5 gouge, not too hollow, not too flat. Use it to work on the chin. Make clean cuts, because they need to remain on the chin, and should not be sanded away later.

*Figure 113. I usually start with a deep frown. Draw some lines on the forehead, to see the effect.*

*Figure 114. Some wood is cut away outside of the triangle, lowering the eyebrows to the nose.*

*Figure 115. The eyes before I reshaped them.*

*Figure 116. After the eyes are reshaped they are smaller and the tear bags more striking.*

You may also use a number 5 gouge to work on the triangle on the forehead. Likewise, make nice, clean cuts that shouldn't be sanded away later. Make the triangle, going down to the nose, pushing down the eyebrows (**Figure 114**). Remove the wood on the outside of the triangle, above the eyebrows, but also make the inside of the triangle uneven.

The frowns and furrows in the forehead give the whole carving a troubled expression (**Figure 115**).

Looking at the carving, I decided the expression is too angry, and not sad enough. The reason is that the eyes are too large. When you cry, they become much smaller, and I intended to carve them small. But now I think they still are too big. So, back to work. I remove the upper eyelid completely, and in addition I cut the eye deeper. I can easily do this. There is enough wood, and the effect on the whole eye will only be beneficial. The deeper the eye lies in this sad face, the more expression they get. And the eye cover fold becomes larger, which is good for a sad face.

And this is the result. Compare these two photographs: (**Figure 115** and **Figure 116**).

# 9. Tidying up and removing the base.

Still, I think the face looks a bit too angry, I want more sadness. So I made yet another change. I take back the lower lip and prolong it, so the mouth is more crying. Compare the mouth in the two photographs at right (**Figure 117**).

Have another look at your sphere. Does it still need to be rounded? You can make the base smaller. This makes it much easier to refine the shape of the sphere.

If you're content with the spherical shape, you can tidy the carving up. Tidying up means you have to take away the tool marks on the sphere. In this case leave the gouge cuts on the forehead and chin.

Taking the tool marks off your carving will help you save time while sanding. My piece of pear is hard, and it would take me a long time to sand away gouge marks. Therefore I will make sure the sphere has as few marks as possible.

To remove the base read the section on removing the base for the laughing face on page 58

*Figure 117. Another change, the lower lip is cut back and made to look longer, being part of the skin pulling it aside.*

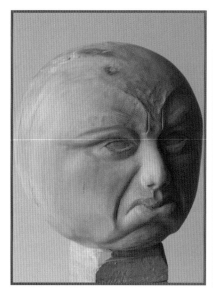

*Figure 118. The face loses depth and color when you are sanding.*

*Figure 119. You can leave tool marks on the spot between the lines of the triangle on the forehead.*

*Figure 120. The sanding is finished.*

# 10. Sanding

This piece of pear is really beautiful and I want the sphere to be soft and show all the beautiful lines of the wood.

This means I have some sanding to do. Pear is hard, and the sanding will take longer than for a piece of lime. I decided to sand the sphere with a machine. I prefer to do that outside, with the wind blowing in the right direction, away from me. When I use the machine I start with 100 grit sandpaper.

There are a lot of sanding machines on the market. I often use a small triangle-shaped sanding machine, sometimes called a detail sander. I can hold it in one hand and turn the sphere with the other hand, always keeping an overview on the shape. With a machine it is easy to alter the nice round shape into something flat or oval. Concentrate on the form. After having removed the obvious marks on the wood, I end by sanding by hand.

Don't use a machine to sand the face. You will not be able to work accurately enough with a machine. You need to preserve the character of your carving.

In the chapter on sanding the laughing face, you can read more details about sanding.

I start with 100 grit for the face and go up to 320 grit (**Figure 118**).

After sanding, carve in some of

the details again. Give the furrows a fresh cut, and cut in the eye again, where it disappears under the eyelids, to give it more depth. You might need to undercut the nasolabial furrow if it hasn't got enough depth.

I do not sand the chin, lips, eyebrows and a small part of the forehead, the spot between the lines of the triangle (**Figure 119**).

When I finish sanding, the face looks like **Figure 120**.

# 11. Finishing with oil

I finish the crying face with oil.

I apply Chinese tung oil mixed with orange oil (70% tung oil, 30% orange oil). The finishing process is described in Chapter 10.

The oil darkens the pear remarkably, especially around the knots near the top of the sphere. The triangle on the forehead remains a shade lighter (**Figure 121**).

*Figure 121. The oil darkens the pear remarkably, especially around the knots in the piece. This is how it looks after one coat of tung oil mixed with orange oil.*

**Tip:** Don't forget your coffee, or tea, break. It refreshes your body ànd your mind. You will work faster after a break. I often use breaks to browse in woodcarving magazines and art books, always looking for new ideas for the next carving.

Chapter 15

# Step by step to a softly smiling face

Even when you smile softly, quite a lot of muscles move in your face. The changes are not as striking as in a loudly laughing face, but your muscles move in the same way (**Figure 122**).

The most import change when you go from a serious look to a smile is in your cheeks. The cheeks are being pushed closer to the eyes. However, as you are only softly smiling your eyes do not become very small, like they do in a loudly laughing face. In a softly smiling face I like to make the eyes big and beautiful, which will enhance the soft smile. The pupil in the eye will be very important for a softly smiling face. You do not want the figure to stare and look harsh. So we will need to give the eye a soft expression.

Do not make the mouth too small. Give it full lips. People with very narrow lips always look less happy. That is because a bitter or sour person presses his lips together so that they become narrower. The mouth is closed, but the lips are not pressed together.

The muscles around the mouth pull the edges of the mouth upward and deeper; the nasolabial furrow deepens slightly.

I advise you to read the chapter on what happens in a loudly laughing face. It is the more exaggerated form of what you will be carving now.

Stand in front of a mirror and smile softly. Look at your cheeks and mouth. Another very interesting way to know your face is to sit down and put your fingertips on your cheeks. Now smile. Do this several times, and try to find out which part of your face changes, and what doesn't move at all.

*Figure 122. What happens in a softly smiling face?*

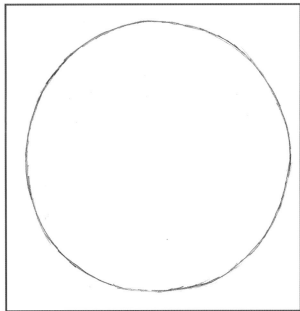

*Figure 123. Draw a circle by hand.*          *Figure 124. A front view of a smiling face.*

# 1. Make a drawing

To start you need a circle. I always draw it by hand because I do not want the circle to be too perfect.

You can make a drawing as big as your wood, of you can just draw it any dimension you like and then make photocopies in the exact dimensions.

Start with the easiest drawing, a circle. This is your side and front view for the first stage (**Figure 123**).

Now you can make a simple drawing of the head as seen from the top. Copy the flattened circle, mark a central line and draw a nose on the outside of the circle. The nose must be symmetrical, as much space on the left of your central line as on the right. Draw the nose big enough; give yourself some extra space in case something goes wrong.

Next follows a more detailed plan, a drawing of the front view of a softly smiling face. It is a plan. It shows the important lines for you to carve; it is not a piece of art, just a plan to work with. You can copy this plan, but you can also try to draw a smiling face by yourself. You could make the nose broader, longer, the mouth a bit further away from the nose, or closer to it... You could make the forehead smaller, or the chin smaller. No face is ever the same; your choice is as good as mine (**Figure 124**).

A profile view of a smiling face looks like this. Only the nose is really sticking out of the sphere. The following areas are lower than the surface of the sphere: the nose bridge and the area going up to the eyebrows, the philtrum, and the space under the lower lip just above the chin. The eyebrows and the chin are on the surface of the sphere

# 2. Choose and prepare your wood

For this smiling spherical head I chose a piece of lime. A fine grained piece, no knots or cracks in this pale piece of wood.

Make sure you do not select a piece that will have flaws, knots or splits in the forehead. A smiling, happy person has no wrinkles or unevenness on his forehead. An uneven rugged forehead makes a smile look sarcastic.

Take a good look at all the peculiarities of your wood. You need to know where the face will be before you start to work.

I took a piece of a large beam with a thickness of 4½ inches (11.5 cm). So, I can make a sphere with a maximum diameter of 4½ inches.

For the spherical face I need a piece of wood 4½ inches (11.5 cm) wide, 5 inches (13 cm) thick and 6½ inches (16.5 cm) long.

The piece of wood is rectangular because I need extra wood for the nose on the face. I need the 4½ inches for the sphere and ½ inch for the nose. A total of 5 inches (13 cm) thick. As for the length, I chose about 2 inches (5 cm) for the base. This means the lime is 6½ inches (16.5 cm) high.

In **Figure 125** you can easily see how the tree has grown, and where the piece I have chosen, comes from. At the backside of the sphere, you see the sapwood of the tree. In

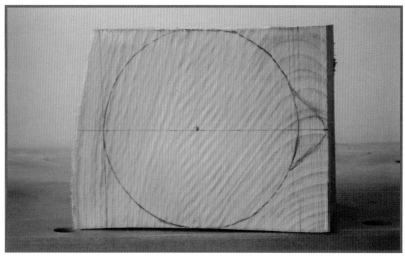

Figure 125. A piece of lime with sapwood but also with very beautiful grain.

Figure 126. A profile view. Notice the base, it is not in the center, but placed more to the back of the sphere.

linden you hardly see the difference in color between sapwood and heartwood. You can feel it though; the wood is more difficult to cut. You will very often need to cut across the grain. But I decided to use this piece because I like the grain for the face, and the back of the sphere is less important.

The piece is not very straight, so I put all the lines and drawings on it, to make sure I will have a correct start (**Figure 126**).

The base is a square of about 2 inches (5 cm), and is not exactly in the middle. I placed the base more to the back of the sphere, to get more room for the face.

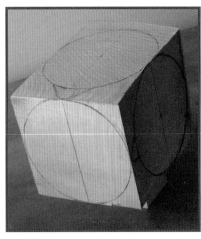

Figure 127. All of the wood outside of the top view can be removed.

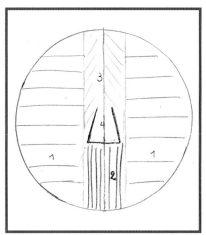

Figure 128. How to make a nose. 1. Remove the wood on both sides of the nose. 2. Remove the redundant wood under the nose. 3. Shape the wood into a triangle. 4. Make the triangle slope down to the face.

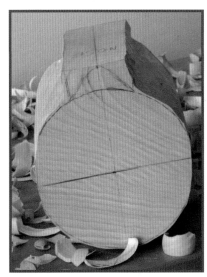

Figure 129. Enough wood is left for the nose.

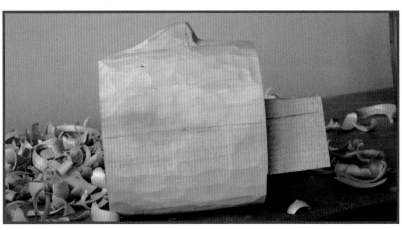

Figure 130. A triangle sloping down to the face, this is a nose.

# 3. Make a cylinder with space for a nose

Draw the plan of the top view on top of your wood. Proceed as for the loudly laughing face in chapter 9.

Draw a central line starting on the top and come down on the side where the face will be (**Figure 127**).

First make a cylinder. Remove all of the wood on the outside of the top view drawing. Remove the corners first. Use a large hollow gouge, for example a Pfeil number 8/16 to 20. You can proceed with a flatter gouge, for example a number Pfeil 3/20.

On the face side you can work around the nose in three stages as this drawing shows (**Figure 128**).

First remove the wood on both sides of the nose using a U-tool, for example a number 11/7 (or even larger, up to 11/15, could be used). Cut away enough so you can make the face spherical at the same time (**Figure 129**).

Next draw the nose on your piece and carve the part under the nose away. Again use a U-tool. The third step is to cut the wood that is still there into a triangle.

The last stage is to take away the abundant wood and carve it into the form of a nose. From the highest point of the nose make the wood slope down to the face. You can do that with an almost flat, broad gouge, number 3/20 or 2/20 (**Figure 130**).

# 4. Make the cylinder into a sphere

Now you can carve the cylinder into a sphere. Mark the center of the circle on the top and three sides with an X (not on the face). You can connect the X's with a line, to visualize the middle of your circle on the sides.

Start removing wood on the corners. Work your way up from each X to the central point on the top. This allows you to cut with the grain and avoid end grain as much as possible. At the bottom you can only remove wood until the base gets in the way.

When you cut away corners there is a flat space remaining on top. Always make this flat space round. The more wood you remove, the smaller the circle should become. Always keep the central point in the middle. Work on all sides at the same time, top and bottom. The sphere is finished when you have no flat spots left (**Figure 131**).

If the nose is too big it is difficult to round the part above the nose. You can remove some of the wood from the top of the nose with a U-gouge, thus creating more room to make the carving spherical on the face side (**Figure 132**).

*Figure 131. Changing the cylinder into a sphere. The circle on top must become smaller and smaller until there is no flat space left.*

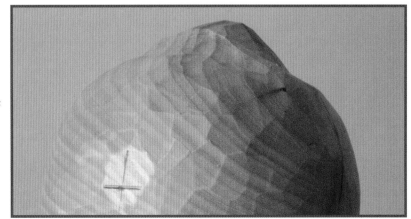

*Figure 132. Refine the top of the nose with a U-gouge so you can make the forehead spherical.*

*Figure 133. Draw nose and eyebrows.*

*Figure 134. Cut along the eyebrows and the nose.*

# 5. The nose

Redraw the central line and draw the nose and two brow lines on your carving (**Figure 133**).

As the piece is not flat anymore, you cannot just copy the drawing of the front view of the face.

Measure the distance of the eyebrows from the top and the distance between the eyebrows. Also measure the width of the nose in the smallest and widest places. With the help of these measured points draw the line from the eyebrow to the bottom of the nose. Do not pin the drawing on the nose, the highest point. Refine the nose. And carve with a number 11/5 gouge along the nose line, from the bottom of the nose to the point where the grain changes direction. This is also the deepest point, the corner side of the eye near the nose. Next you need to come down with the number 11/5 gouge along the brow line. Start in the middle of the brow line (**Figure 134**).

After repeating this a few times you develop a nose bridge. At the same time, remove some of the wood on the left and right sides where the eyes need to be developed. In my drawing, the highest point of the eyeball, that is, the highest point of the pupil, is ⅜ inch (8 mm) lower than the nose bridge. The eyelids are about ¼ inch (6 mm) lower than the nose bridge. Draw a line at the height of the nose bridge, from nose to the cheekbone. Drop this line with a U-gouge until it is ¼ inch (6 mm) lower than the nose bridge, and the height of the eyelid, at its highest point.

Look at this picture: **Figure 135**. The left side has only been cut in along the eyebrow and nose line. On the right, a cut has been made and the eye cover fold slopes down to the U-cut.

Remove wood from the cheeks, so that the nose connects with the cheeks. The sides of the nose slope down to the cheeks (**Figure 136**).

Now work on the bottom of the nose. The highest point of a nose is not completely at the bottom. Take wood off from the highest point, down to the philtrum and upper part of the mouth.

In this face I want a fine, slim nose. The nose wings shouldn't attract too much attention. I will finish the nose wing in the next stage when I am working on the nasolabial furrow and the part around the mouth.

You can now begin to make a hole for the nostrils. You can complete those when working on the nasolabial furrow (**Figure 137**).

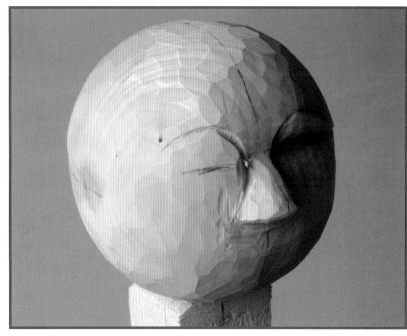

*Figure 135. The left side has a cut along the eyebrow and nose line. On the right, a cut has been made and the eye cover fold slopes down to the U-cut.*

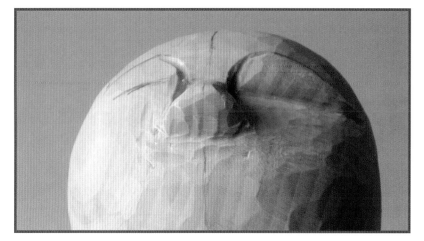

*Figure 136. Lower the cheeks. The right side has been lowered, the left is yet to be done.*

*Figure 137. Progress on the nose and nostrils.*

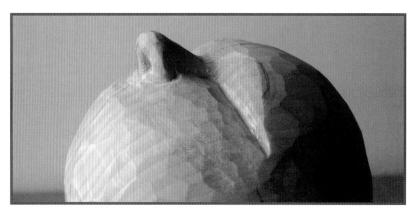

Figure 138. Cut in the nasolabial furrow.

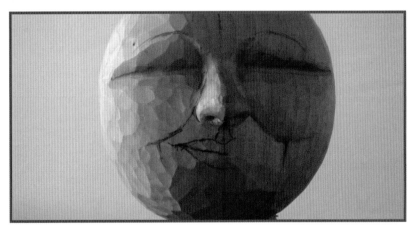

Figure 139. The right corner of the mouth has been dropped.

# 6. Carving the nasolabial furrow

Draw the nasolabial furrow and mouth.

Carving on the nasolabial furrow means you will also be working at the same time on the global round form of the mouth, the cheek and also the bottom of the nose wings and nostrils.

A softly smiling cheek is round and slightly pushed upwards. The furrow is not very visible around the nose, and sort of flows into the cheeks.

Find a gouge that matches the form of the nose wing and cut in (**Figure 138**). The nose wings need to be undercut on the sides. Doing this, you start to create the furrow, which starts just above the nosewing. The furrow in a softly smiling face is not very deep. It is the line that separates nose, cheek and mouth.

Remove some of the wood behind the nose wing and use a small hollow gouge to cut in the line of the furrow, going down to the corners of the mouth.

The mouth is much more convex than we usually imagine. Think of those plaster models dentists make of people's teeth. This means you have to make the corners of the mouth drop deep enough (**Figure 139**). You can do this by lowering the part of the mouth coming from the middle, the highest point of the lips (exactly on the central line), going deeper to the corners of the mouth.

Cut the furrow in again and again, so you can make the corners of the mouth drop deep enough to make the right convex form (**Figure 140**).

On the other side of the furrow lies the cheek. The wood on that side needs to be rounded into the furrow.

# 7. Carving the mouth and lips

Carving a beautiful smile, with beautiful lips, is quite difficult. Have another look at the drawing of lips and their expression of emotion. A smile means that the corners of the mouth are slightly upwards (**Figure 141**).

Draw the philtrum and upper lip on your carving. The philtrum is a hollow spot going from the bottom of the nose to the top of the upper lip.

Find the gouge matching the bottom line of the upper lip. Cutting in the line between the upper and bottom lip is very important to give the mouth a pleasing and correct form.

In the middle of the lip I stab in lightly with a number 5/8 gouge, a slightly hollow gouge that has the same shape as the upper line of the upper lip. On the left and the right of this cut, use the same gouge, but turn it upside-down. Further to the corner, to the left and right, use a flatter gouge and follow the line of your drawing. A number 3 has the right form here.

Cutting in the middle of the mouth gets you started on shaping

*Figure 140. Draw the upper lip and philtrum. The corners of the mouth and furrow are deep enough.*

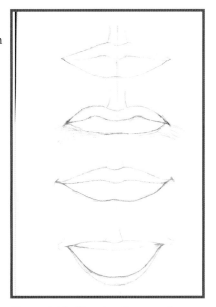

*Figure 141. Drawing the mouth.*

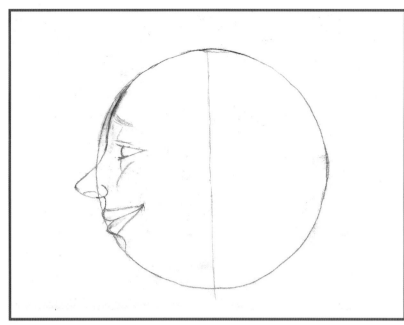

*Figure 142. Profile drawing of the softly smiling face.*

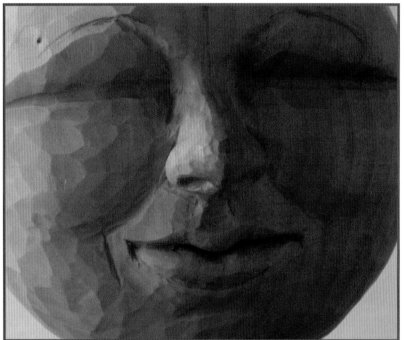

*Figure 143. Developing the smiling lips.*

both lips. Let the upper lip slope down to the cut you've just made. Do the same with the bottom lip. The drawing of the profile shows you the shape you should achieve (**Figure 142**).

In order to shape the lips you need to re-cut the middle line between the lips several times. Always use the same gouges as used the first time.

For the left and right side of the bottom lip, start working in the corners of the mouth. The bottom lip joins the upper lip in the corner, but lies a bit deeper. Use a small, very hollow gouge (number 11/1), to cut in at each corner. Lower the bottom lip slightly at the corner, so it joins the upper lip on a lower level (**Figure 143**).

To make the mouth smile be certain that both corners of the upper lip go up. Give a little cut with a small, lightly curved, gouge on the left and right of the lips. This cut is not really the upper lip itself, but a line that runs a bit further than the lip in an upwards turn. This small crease is what makes the mouth smiling.

Under the bottom lip, mark the line between mouth and chin with a cut of a U-gouge, not too close to the bottom of the lip. This face has no chin, but you need to reduce the part under the lip. This makes the lower lip stand out. Cut the part that could be a chin back to the shape of the sphere.

# 8. Carving the cheeks and eyes

Mark the eyeball on the carving and cut in the line near the cheek with a U-gouge. Don't be afraid to damage the cheeks, there is still too much wood near the eyes.

Carve the cheekbones. This means removing wood at the outside of the eyes, thus lowering the cheekbones. There is still too much bulging wood (**Figure 144**).

At the same time, also with a hollow gouge, cut along the line of the eyebrows and lower the eye cover fold.

Remove the wood in the triangle, as noted in **Figure 145**.

We have to shape the eyeball further. Look at the profile. If the whole eyeball is too high, it needs to be lowered (**Figure 146**).

For a smiling face the bottom of the cheeks must be round. Turn a flat gouge upside down and start from the middle of the cheek and cut a smooth curve down to the nasolabial furrow. Cut in again with a U-gouge, going from the nasolabial furrow to the outside of the cheek in a nice upward curve. The cheeks need to be round, but not bulging like in a loudly laughing face.

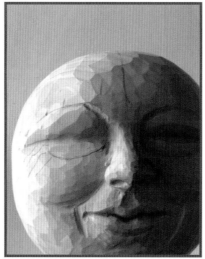

*Figure 144. Removing wood near the cheekbones.*

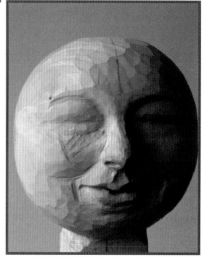

*Figure 145. Remove the wood in the triangle.*

*Figure 146. Working on the eyeball.*

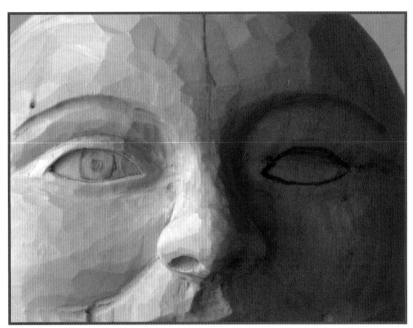

Figure 147. You need to make the eye look like part of a sphere.

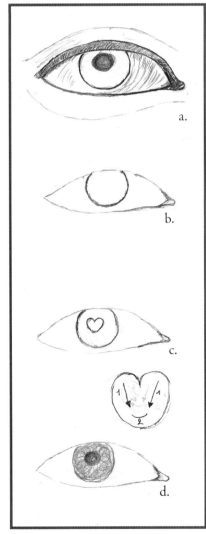

Figure 148. Eye details.

# 9. The eyes in detail

If the eyeball is lowered enough, you can draw the eyes on. Measure the distance from the nose and the dimension of the eye itself. Draw it on the carving and have a good look at it before you start cutting the eye in. Make sure the eye is not too small or too narrow. The eyes are important, you want to create a clear look, a happy eye.

With gouges that match the form of the eye, stab in the line you drew. Use the same gouges for both eyes. For the upper eyelid, tilt the gouge slightly to undercut the eyelid. Lower the eye for about $1/10$ of an inch (1 to 1.5 mm) with a small, almost flat gouge (such as a number 2). Do not make the upper and lower sides too round. Think of the complete eyeball, it disappears under the eyelids, you need to make the eye look like a part of a sphere. Remember the left and right corners go much deeper (**Figure 147**).

On the outside of the eye the lower eyelid folds under the upper eyelid.

The upper eyelid is heavier than the lower one. That is because we cannot carve eyelashes. To make up for that, we make the eyelid more striking.

Carve in along the line of the upper eyelid with a small hollow gouge. Remember there's the eyeball underneath, let the shape of the eyelid follow the form of the eyeball.

For the bottom eyelid, carve along the eye line about $1/8$ inch (3 mm) lower with a hollow gouge. You need to broaden that groove to shape the lower eyelid.

Don't forget, a spherical head is not realistic. The sphere often slopes backward too much for a normal eyebrow, eye cover fold, and normal forehead.

One of the most difficult things in carving a face is to make an eye look, to make it lively, and thus make the whole face come alive. There are different possibilities, and some are more suitable for certain expressions than others.

In traditional woodcarving you often find eyes without an iris or pupil. Such an eye gives a very distant, and absent, look. A face with an eye like that doesn't really speak to you. I do use it sometimes if I do not want to attract too much attention to the eyes, or if I want a person to look distracted or dreamy, or for the sad face, an eye full of tears (**Figure 148**).

Another possibility is to show the iris in the eye, but not the pupil (**Figure 148b**). For smiling people you can use this kind of eye. Draw an iris on the eye. Never draw a total circle in the eye. This will make the face look extremely surprised, or startled. Look at your own eyes, or at other people. Normally you never see the complete circle of the iris. A part of it disappears under the upper eyelid, or under the lower eyelid if you look down.

Before you cut in anything in the eyeball, sand the eyeball. It will be impossible to sand it after you have cut in an iris and/or pupil.

Use a matching gouge (a number 9) to cut in the circle line of the iris. With a small almost flat gouge make the iris into a little round ball within the eyeball. This gives a clear, but not too intense look. Do not make it too round or too ball-shaped.

If you want a rather soft look, also not too intense, but more direct than the previous solution, you can add a small heart-shaped hole in the iris (**Figure 148c**). This heart-shape hole casts a small shadow and gives the eye more expression (**Figure 149**).

I carve this little shape with a small U-gouge such as a number 11/1. Please try it out on another piece first. Cut from the top of the heart to the bottom, left and right side of the heart and at the bottom cut the fibers (**Figure 150**).

For a more intense look you can make a hole in the eye for the iris, not too deep, more like a shallow soup bowl (**Figure 148d**). Hollow the iris out with a small hollow gouge and try not to damage the eye or to make the iris too hollow. Practice it on another piece of wood. It is difficult to make a clean, hollow iris. You will also need to sand it.

In the hollow iris you can yet make another little hole for the pupil. Drill this hole in the iris for an even deeper and more intense look. On an angry face you need a very hard look, and the hollow iris with hollow pupil can give you that.

Figure 149. The eyes can give the face a totally different expression.

Figure 150. The iris with a heart shaped pupil.

*Figure 151. Rounding off the bottom of the sphere.*

# 10. Tidying up and removing the base

Do this by daylight, in the morning, when you are not tired.

Maybe you need to refine some features. Look at the mouth. Is the line that parts the two lips neat? Are the corners of the mouth smiling? Are the nostrils finished?

If you are happy with the features of your smiling face, you can tidy the carving with a gouge, and prepare it for sanding.

Take a large almost flat gouge, number 2/25 or 2/30. Remove any ugly cuts.

The base has to be removed.

Use a large gouge, a number 2, and a U-tool, number 11, and your mallet. Cut in, following the shape of the sphere and remove wood from the base. Make it smaller by repeating this maneuver until you can remove the base completely. The idea is to make the lower part of the sphere round (**Figure 151**).

# 11. Sanding

I sand this smiling face. It will look much happier when all the tool marks are gone. A smiling person has no worries, so has no wrinkles on the forehead or cheeks.

I start with 100 grit for the sphere and 120 grit for the face. Use good quality sanding paper. I prefer to work with sanding strips of cloth.

You have to go through all the grits, from coarse to fine.

Do not sand away the beautiful facial details, but try to enhance the important smiling features. This means you must be very careful around the laughing mouth. Don't take the corners of the mouth down. Sand the cheeks going up, not going down. On **Figure 152** I have marked with arrows the direction you should sand.

Wipe off the sanding dust regularly to give you some appreciation of your progress.

Fold the sandpaper to work in the furrows. For a very narrow or small furrow such as under the eye and between the eye and cheek, just fold the paper in two.

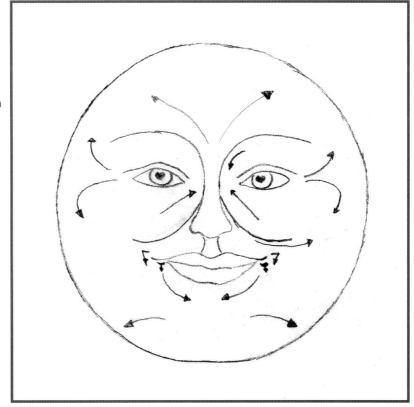

Figure 152. The arrows show you where to sand and in what direction.

Figure 153. The left nasolabial furrow has been widened a bit.

Be very careful if you sand the eyelids.

The left nasolabial furrow starts a bit too close to the nose, so I widened the furrow by taking away some wood in the furrow with a small hollow gouge. To make the cheeks join the mouth again I used a flat gouge turned upside-down and made a smooth cut downwards. (**Figure 153** and **Figure 154**).

After sanding, your carving looks rather dull, colorless, and without depth. Carve in some details again. The upper eyelid. The little furrows around the mouth. The eyeball where it disappears under the eyelids. I usually do not sand the lips.

Figure 154. The sanding is completed.

# 12. Finishing

I like to finish a carving with oil. Just oil, nothing more. But there is a great variety of oils on the market.

For this softly smiling face I want the lines of the wood to be present, but not too conspicuous and I do not want the lime to darken too much.

Therefore I chose lemon oil for this face. The lemon oil I use is made from lemongrass oil, and gives a matte finish. It smells very good too.

The lemon oil will not make the lime as yellow as the tung oil does. But you have to like the really very matte finish. Give each coat 24 hours to dry.

When you start to apply the oil the dullness of the face disappears immediately (**Figure 156**). I use a brush to apply the oil. This allows me to get oil in between the lips and in the nostrils, and in the eyes.

**Figure 157** shows our face after two coats of oil. I will apply another four coats.

Afterward I finish with a bit of olive oil on a waterproof sandpaper. You need a very fine abrasive, 600 grit or more. I rub softly all over the carving and finish with a soft cloth, to take all the oil away.

The result will be a very smooth and soft carving, ready to be touched. I noticed that with these faces one of the first things people want to do is touch the wood, feel the face. They are always pleasantly surprised at the very soft feel of the wood.

*Figure 156. The dullness of the sanded wood disappears the instant you apply oil.*

*Figure 157. With two coats of oil, the face begins to look finished. I will apply several more coats, to protect the wood and create the sheen I want.*

Chapter 16

# Overview of faces with emotions

The range of emotions is incredibly vast. If you start carving faces and you like it, you'll be having fun for many years to come.

To carve emotions you need to know the basics of the anatomy of a face. If you do not know that, it will be harder to notice and recognize the differences that define an emotion.

A good start to carve emotions is to look at people. Photographs and books with portraits are very helpful. Sometimes it is difficult to find photographs of people with ugly emotions, like madness, deception, and disappointment. Have a look in the books that are issued yearly with the best photos of the year. These books often feature people in extreme situations, which are reflected in their faces.

If you have never carved an emotion, start with an easy face, a face without a lot of emotion. You can learn the important features in a face such as the depth of eyes, the formation of the mouth and nose.

Here are some general rules that you can always apply if you want to show an emotion in a face.

- a clean forehead means a happy person. As soon as you put wrinkles in a forehead you give an idea of the more ugly emotions like anger, worry, fear, or sadness.

- the eyebrows move together with the forehead, and are a very clear indication of an emotion. Eyebrows pushed down, angry, or sad. Eyebrows pulled up, surprised, horrified, and frightened.

Figure 158. Compare this head, 10¼ inches (26 cm), with Figure 167 on page 117.

*Figure 159. The **Dreamer**; In lime, diameter about 5½ inches (14 cm).*

- the nasolabial furrow always moves along with each emotion. It is very flexible, and a very important indication of an emotion. You always have to know what this furrow does, before you start to carve, in order to make the emotion in your carving work.

- a cheek is also a good indication of our feelings. Chubby cheeks pushed upwards, happy feelings. Cheeks going down, pulled downwards, rather hollow, the person is angry, sad, or worried.

- the mouth is one of the most flexible parts of our face, and the emotion comes pouring out of a mouth. You can scream out of horror, mouth wide open. You can laugh loudly, mouth wide open. Quite different emotions, but we recognize the difference immediately.

- the eyes are the most difficult features to carve. It is very difficult to make carved eyes look and express the emotion you want them to. The best way is to use different irises and pupils to indicate an emotion. You should also take a good look at what happens to the eyelids.

Changes in the forehead, cheeks and mouth can change the expression in a face dramatically, from laughing to crying, from happiness to anger.

A rather easy face is a dreamy person, someone contemplating something, with the eyes closed. You can learn the right proportions in a face, and you do not have to carve eyes! (**Figure 159**) I carved

A Dreamer. The person could be asleep, dreaming about nice things, but could also be awake, just thinking about something nice. I gave this face a very soft smile (you can compare it to the softly smiling face). There is not much happening in this face. The cheeks are pushed up very slightly, because of the mild smile. The nasolabial furrow is not too conspicuous. The forehead is smooth and even. This dreamer has no worries. The closed eyes mean you don't have to make the carving look.

A troubled person has all the opposite features. The forehead is uneven, with some furrows. The eyebrows are pushed down, towards the nose. The cheeks are rather flat or even hollow. The mouth narrows the nasolabial furrow. This mouth is narrow; the corners are going down. You can give an unhappy or worried person narrow lips to enhance the feeling of unhappiness. Bags under the eyes do the same thing (**Figure 160**).

An angry face is close to a troubled face. The forehead uneven with furrows, eyebrows are going down to the nose bridge. The eye cover fold lies close to the eye. And very important, the corners of the mouth go down. These features can also be carved into a very small spherical head. Just go for the most important details. This little angry head has a diameter of 2 inches (5 cm) (**Figure 161**).

**Figure 162** is another crying, spherical head. Compared to the sad spherical face I described, this one really is only crying and very unhappy. In this face you see no anger, only sadness. I used the split in the wood to make the face look even more unhappy. The crack

Figure 160. Troubled, worried, and very unsure. A face in elm, diameter about 8½ inches (22 cm).

Figure 161. A small, angry, spherical head, 2 inches (5 cm), in cherry.

*Figure 162. This crying face was made in cherry, supplied as a branch from a friend's garden. The diameter is about 5 inches (13 cm).*

*Figure 163. "Pffff....", in lime/linden, diameter 1½ inches (4 cm).*

*Figure 164. Surprise! Cherry, diameter 4¾ inches (12 cm).*

opens in winter, because of the central heating, and becomes smaller in the summer, when there is more moisture in the room. Looking at this face makes you feel like crying too (**Figure 162**).

In a disappointed face the mouth is prominent. But disappointment is a complex emotion, and you can do a lot of things with a face to express disappointment. Whatever you choose, it is not a very happy feeling, so don't let the cheeks go up nor should the corners of the mouth point upwards. A disappointed person could be sulking, if so, push the lower lip forward. I made a 1½ inch (4 cm) spherical face saying "Pffffff!! I've had it!" (**Figure 163**)

Surprise is also a nice emotion to carve. Surprise can come very near to the emotion of horror, horrified surprise. A surprised person raises his eyebrows, they go way up his forehead, and the eyes are opened wide. It is the only time when you can see the whole iris in someone's eye. Make sure to use this and your face will indeed look very surprised. The mouth says 'oh' for a suprise that is not frightening (**Figure 164**).

Compare the surprise in the previous face to the horrified suprise in this little head (**Figure 165**). You can clearly see that he didn't get a nice surprise, on the contrary, what he sees is rather frightening. The open mouth speaks for itself, the person is baffled with what he sees, and he doesn't like it. The eyebrows are raised, the eyes wide open.

If you know what happens in a face for an emotion, you can start using this knowledge. If you alter some details, you get very different faces.

I have two examples of loudly laughing faces, and both quite different from the one described in this book, **Figure 165** and **Figure 167**. One face is small, about 2¼ inches (6 cm) diameter. I carved the upper teeth, but not the lower teeth. I gave the eyes two small pupils. The other laughing face is much bigger with a diameter of 10 inches (26 cm) and is in lime/linden. I carved all the teeth, but in a very easy way, not too much detail. Nor did I give the eyes an iris, I wanted to draw all the attention to the mouth and chubby cheeks. The same emotion, but a different result.

A difficult emotion to carve is the face of someone who is winking. Winking is the effect of a happy emotion. You never wink when you are angry or in a bad mood. Winking comes with a smile. This face is very asymmetrical. The left side is smiling softly but happily, on the right side the face is pulled up toward the winking eye. A winking eye is a closed eye, but not the way your eye is closed when you sleep or dream. It is an active closed eye. Closing the eye takes only a second, and it is that one particular second you are carving. Closing the eye pulls the cheek higher and makes it bulge more than the other one. The corner of the mouth on the winking side goes up, and there are some extra laughing wrinkles on the winking side (**Figure 166**).

Figure 165. Not a nice surpise! Only 1½ inches (4 cm) in diameter, of zapatero (Maracaibo boxwood, Gossypiospermum praecox).

Figure 166. A small winking sphere in zapatero, 4 centimeters.

Figure 167. **Loudly Laughing** is a 2¼ inch (6 cm) diameter sphere of cherry.

# Chapter 17

# Design: what is it?

Your design is your plan, your drawing for the subject you are going to carve.

But design means much more. It is the style you choose to work in, your own personal style, or a style you have discovered in furniture, architecture, paintings, or decorations. It can also be a combination of the two: you saw something you liked very much and you adapted it to your own ideas.

Maybe this sounds difficult, but it comes with practice. Maybe it sounds far-fetched, but it is not. Try it and you will see. By trial and error you can develop your own ideas, style, and design. But you have to want to try and dare. And try and dare again.

A copy of something can be extremely well done, but it remains forever a copy. However, you can learn to add your own ideas and your own concepts. I purposely use the word learn because I am convinced that everyone can learn to develop an idea, a concept of his own, and a wonderful design.

Design sounds like a modern word, but is in fact a concept that has been with us since the dawn of time.

I found a striking example in the village of Grimbergen, where I have lived for eight years. There is a Norbertine abbey, founded in 1128, and a beautiful baroque church. Construction began on St. Servatius church in 1660. They stopped working in 1725 because there was no more money. The exterior still looks extremely unfinished (**Figure 168**). But the interior of this baroque basilica is extraordinarily

*Figure 168. Begun in 1660, the exterior of the St. Servatius church still looks very unfinished.*

beautiful (**Figure 169**).

A host of wonderful wood sculptures are to be found in the basilica. These sculptures are centuries old, and are proof that design is not a modern concept. Have a look at the photos of the misericords, the wood sculptures underneath the pew seats. Many are variations on the Green Man theme. For me they show how the sculptor in the 17th century let his imagination work within an existing theme (**Figure 170**, next page).

*Figure 169. Built in the 17th century, St. Servatius was declared a bascilica by Pope John Paul in 1999.*

*Figure 170. The misericord carvings are all variations on the Green Man theme.*

Figure 171. The St. Servatius basilica contains many unusual carvings.

Figure 172. A wonderful facial study from the basilica.

# Creativity and creation

What does the word creativity mean? You can see the word creation in creativity. Creativity is the ability to create something new. A simple, although not exhaustive, definition could be, to produce new, novel ideas.

You have to do some creative thinking to develop a good, fresh idea. What is the difference between thinking and creative thinking? Why can't we produce creative ideas all day long?

It is a misconception that only some people are creative, and others aren't, that some were born creative, others not. This is wrong. You can learn to be creative. You can learn a language, you can learn mathematics, you can learn to be creative.

Don't believe that creativity is only for artistic people. Some people see artistic as the opposite of realistic. Creativity is not only for softies. Many companies hold creative brainstorming sessions to help make the organization work more efficiently and keep jobs interesting for their employees. In the professional world, creativity and innovation are complementary.

The very first step in this process of creativity is to realize you need time. The next step is finding that time. I know, the urge to start carving right away is great. I know from experience that I just want to get started, take those gouges and work in this wonderful material called wood.

But, there always is a but: you cannot start without thinking first. What will you carve? What do you want to express?

There must be some moments during a day that you can use to sit and just think. If there are no such moments in your day then you must make them. Pick a time to think. This thinking will not take a whole day, but the quality of your thinking is important.

# How does the brain think?

Thinking is the engine of the creative process. What happens in the brain when we think? Our brain structure is incredibly complex. The brain consists of about a 100 billion neurons. Each neuron has a cell body with branching dendrites, up to 100,000 per neuron. Dendrites receive messages. Every neuron also has one axon, a long extension of the nerve cell that takes information away from the cell body.

Thinking is the interaction between all these cells. Information is being sent from neuron to neuron. A path is created by our brain cells and after a while patterns are created. The signals start to follow the same route, from neuron to neuron. In our lives, this is indispensable. Remember when you learned to drive a car. At first it was hard. You had to think about everything, looking at the traffic, watching the traffic signals, applying the brakes, accelerating, and so on. But after a while it became easy. Now you drive without even realizing you are doing so many things at the same time.

We need to realize that when we think, the brain often follows the same, well-known paths and patterns. These patterns facilitate our lives. You can drive, while thinking about other things. But, at the same time these patterns prevent us from being creative, from developing new ideas. Creative thinking means we have to produce new paths resulting in new ideas.

But how can we break our patterns? We need to exercise our brains, just as we do a workout for our muscles. We need to practice the basic skills of creative thinking.

An important skill is the creative observation. We are used to having our own vision of reality. Often we do not use our senses, but just the ideas (formed brain patterns) that we have in our mind. You need to let go of these ideas, and open your mind to renew your vision. Ask yourself, how can I look at this in a different way? Try to observe something you think you already know.

If you try this you must be free of any judgement of yourself, or of any new idea that pops up in your mind. Your mind would prefer to follow the well-known path, but don't give in to it. You need to keep an open mind.

Write down your new perceptions, new ideas, and new feelings. At this moment every one of these is as good as the other. No idea should be thought of as better or of more value.

Now remember the patterns our brain cells like to follow. They are still there. Let's say I want to think about a face. I immediately make some associations such as nose, mouth, eyes, and hair. These are dominant associations. But let's try to make a somewhat less dominant association, such as plastic surgery, dentist, and glasses. Try to be flexible in your associations.

The mind will first provide ordinary and practical ideas. At this point you need to go on thinking. Write down the new things you think of. It may be things or ideas that do not really fit in your usual thinking pattern. They are what you need.

## Your imagination

The next phase is very important for creative thinking, and especially for a sculptor. You need to develop your imagination. You see the word image in imagination. Try to visualize the ideas that came into your mind as images, not as words. It might be more difficult than you think.

In school we were trained to think and learn in words, not in images. The language of words is strong, the language of images almost non-existent. Did you ever need to learn how to imagine something? In schoolbooks images are only there to explain what is written. The words are important. Did a teacher in school, except perhaps your art teacher, ever teach you to see in images? Try to see something that isn't physically before your eyes.

Here is an exercise, think of an apple and look at it in your mind.

Figure 173. A 17th century life-size sculpture in oak. This man shows his emotions, his fear and anxiety.

See the color, the form, feel the texture of the apple (different apples different texture), think of the smell, and notice the feelings that come into your mind.

Look at the next photograph, a sculpture from the 17th century, in the basilica of Grimbergen. What is the first idea that pops into your mind when you see this? Is it man or is it fear or maybe it is anxiety? For me the fear in this sculpture is more important than the man. The sculptor must have had the image of fear in his mind to be able to carve this (**Figure 173**).

The sculptor had to imagine the fear. Not the word fear, but the image, and very important, the feelings, of fear. Whatever you want to carve, the image of your carving must be existing, and even alive, in your mind.

# How to come up with your own idea?

I have mentioned that your imagination is extremely important in creative thinking, but in actual practice, how do you start? How can you produce your own idea?

I usually get started with a lot of books around me, books filled with images of drawings and photographs, books on furniture, art, decoration, jewelry, and pottery. The list is endless. I find them in the library, on the Internet, and in the bookshop.

Books help you to open your mind to new ideas and new forms. Choose the pictures that appeal to you and mark them. It can be pictures of things and forms that you have feelings for. These pictures may produce the emotions of happiness or disgust, mortification, admiration, or fear.

Do you have any ideas that cross your mind when you're looking at the pictures? Write them down immediately. You need to concentrate while going through the books. Try not to go off on a tangent and think about other activities such as shopping or picking the kids up from school. Think about the task at hand.

You can put some music on if you

like. Let your mind travel. Try to find new associations, have new feelings, and new images. New associations don't always come out of the blue. It helps if you write down everything that comes into your mind.

# An exercise in imagination

An example, I open an art book on the Dutch artist M.C.Escher. I possess several books on his work. Maurits Cornelis Escher was an artist in optical illusions and a master in the graphic arts. He combined his skill with his visions and feelings. When I look at some pictures of his works, I always feel admiration, and at the same time I feel a bit scared. For Escher an ordinary square can change into a strange, non-existent animal. You won't find any reproductions of Escher here, I prefer that you go out and look for an Escher art book if you feel tempted or curious. But Escher's strange animals make my imagination soar. Where could this animal live, in what strange world? I try to imagine this world, and it brings up other images, of science fiction movies I have seen and of alarming future worlds. I think of the people that could live in this future world. How would they look? Would they be ugly, or would they be beautiful?

This is only the start of an exercise in imagining, in letting your mind travel. The exercise isn't finished. You must go on and write down the things you think of. You might find a new subject to carve. Your idea of a new being in a strange world, or a non-existent flower or animal. But even if you do not find a new subject to carve, I advise you to keep the notes you have made. You may need them in the future, tomorrow, next week, next year. The new feelings you experienced may bring you new ideas after a couple of hours, or days.

If you have already chosen a subject to carve but want to find a new angle of incidence, this is even more of a challenge. You have to let go of your fixed idea of your chosen subject. Take the freedom to improvise in your mind. Take into account the emotions that you feel.

## Emotions are important

Emotions are important. You should try to put your emotions in your carving, in the act of carving. And subsequently these emotions will be visible in the result. A carving that is the result of a strong or clear image and feelings in your mind will be a good, striking carving.

I usually look for my piece of wood when I already know what I want to carve. You can also work the other way round. Find a piece of wood and wonder what you could make out of this special piece of wood. Does the piece make you think of something or someone, or an emotion? Once again you can have a look in books filled with images and photographs to help you make new associations.

## How did I get the idea of carving spherical emotions?

I put together different ideas and feelings. When I look at art I like simple lines. They give me a feeling of strength.

I also like the lines of the human form, and the emotions emanating from people's faces and movements. An emotion is powerful. Emotions give me the feeling of power.

These two general ideas came together one day. One day, there was a football in our garden that came from the kids next door. I found the ball and looked at it. Suddenly the idea struck me, imagine that you are being kicked around like a football. It must be painful, horrible! Imagine someone hitting you with his foot. It would really hurt, wouldn't it? In my mind I saw a football, with a face in pain.

That was the start of it. A simple but strong form, a sphere, combined with strong emotions. A sphere with a human face filled with emotions.

I am convinced that everyone can learn to use their imagination and that imagination leads to new ideas. At the same time I am convinced that you need to work on it. Ideas do not just fall from the sky. I admit the football fell from the sky, but it only became a creative idea because

I had been thinking about the emotions of simple lines in art, and about human faces and emotions.

## Conclusion

Give yourself some credit and let your mind work and travel. People are creative beings. From the cave dwellers that expressed themselves in their rock art to modern man, the urge to create has been with us from the beginning.

I hope these last chapters may help you in discovering your own creative potential.

*Figure 174.*

# More great woodworking books from Linden Publishing

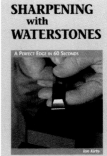

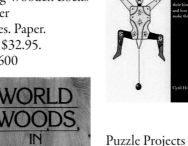
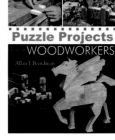
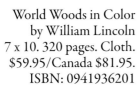

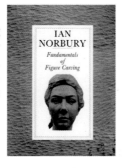

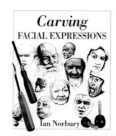